THE CZECHOSLOVAK ACADEMY OF SCIENCES

# ECONOMIC GROWTH
## *in* CZECHOSLOVAKIA

T0347339

# ECONOMIC GROWTH
# *in* CZECHOSLOVAKIA

*An introduction to the theory of economic growth under
socialism, including an experimental application
of Kalecki's model to Czechoslovak statistical data*

Josef Goldmann/Karel Kouba

Routledge
Taylor & Francis Group

LONDON AND NEW YORK

First published 1969 by International Arts and Sciences Press, Inc.

Reissued 2018 by Routledge
2 Park Square, Milton Park, Abingdon, Oxon OX14 4RN
711 Third Avenue, New York, NY 10017, USA

*Routledge is an imprint of the Taylor & Francis Group, an informa business*

Copyright © Josef Goldmann, Karel Kouba, 1969

*Scientific Editor:* Prof. Miroslav Kadlec
*Reviewer:* Doc. Josef Tauchman

No part of this book may be reprinted or reproduced or utilised in any form or by any electronic, mechanical, or other means, now known or hereafter invented, including photocopying and recording, or in any information storage or retrieval system, without permission in writing from the publishers.

Notices
No responsibility is assumed by the publisher for any injury and/or damage to persons or property as a matter of products liability, negligence or otherwise, or from any use of operation of any methods, products, instructions or ideas contained in the material herein.

Practitioners and researchers must always rely on their own experience and knowledge in evaluating and using any information, methods, compounds, or experiments described herein. In using such information or methods they should be mindful of their own safety and the safety of others, including parties for whom they have a professional responsibility.

Product or corporate names may be trademarks or registered trademarks, and are used only for identification and explanation without intent to infringe.

Publisher's Note
The publisher has gone to great lengths to ensure the quality of this reprint but points out that some imperfections in the original copies may be apparent.

Disclaimer
The publisher has made every effort to trace copyright holders and welcomes correspondence from those they have been unable to contact.

A Library of Congress record exists under LC control number: 73402213

ISBN 13: 978-1-138-03805-9 (hbk)
ISBN 13: 978-1-138-03803-5 (pbk)
ISBN 13: 978-1-315-17753-3 (ebk)

# Preface

The main subject of this book is an analysis of economic growth factors, of the major barriers to growth and of the correlation of growth factors under the specific — but not entirely unique — conditions of Czechoslovakia. An attempt is also made to analyse the interrelationship between the strategic parameters of the growth model on the one hand, and the operative model of a socialist economy under changing conditions on the other.

The authors conceive their work as belonging to the new trend of thinking that is endeavouring to comprehend the realities of socialist construction with the aid of an up-to-date tool box of economic research. Application of the growth model to statistical data serves both as a criterion of the effectiveness, under changing conditions, of the administrative-directive system of planned management, and as a contribution to analysing the initial situation from which the Czechoslovak economy is entering the phase of introducing and speeding up realization of a system of planned management on economic lines. In common with the majority of Czechoslovak economists, the present authors are primarily concerned with seeking the optimum trajectory of transition from the economic stagnation of 1961 – 3 to a path of balanced growth, and constructing an economic mechanism capable of ensuring full utilization of the latent reserves existing in Czechoslovakia's comparatively advanced industrial potential.

The outcome of the investigation is handicapped by some unpropitious circumstances, not least being the fact that the theory of economic growth under socialist conditions has only recently been established as a subject in its own right. The work accomplished in this field so far is in the nature of a pioneering probe of the interrelationships among the leading strategic elements of growth in a socialist economy.

Nevertheless, the works of two authors stand out above all others, and some hope of future success can be drawn from their study and application. We have in mind the writings of the Soviet economist G. A. Feldman, dating from the twenties, and of the Polish economist M. Kalecki, from the fifties. While Feldman's articles rank today as rediscovered pioneering work on growth theory in the context of socialist planning, providing a valuable source of ideas for a later pioneer of western growth theories (E. D. Domar), Kalecki's contribution is a product of critical synthesis of contemporary findings yielded by growth theories (including his own), with adjustment to socialist conditions. In view of its synthetic and modern approach, we will adhere to Kalecki's model in our analysis. We anticipate at least two results from this undertaking.

We were primarily interested in Kalecki's growth model because research had demonstrated that by applying it we might arrive at a deeper diagnosis of Czechoslovakia's preceding economic development and of the key problems facing her economy today.

Secondly, we were attracted by the fact that Kalecki and his colleagues had already employed the model in drafting the first version of Poland's long-term plan up to 1975. Today, it is generally recognized that every deeper insight into economic reality provides a stronger guarantee that our projections of future development will be more successful. Moreover, all central planners have learned from experience that the basic problems presented by the contemporary state of the economy and by future development always emerge more clearly during the practical work of planning, that is in drafting long-term plans, than in the course of purely analytical research confined to examining past growth and the present situation.

Furthermore, none-too-happy experiences have taught us that some of the divergent features exhibited by the Czechoslovak economy in comparison with the other socialist countries make it still more urgent that, in line with the changed model of socialist economic operation, some of the out-dated methods of constructing long-term plans should be relinquished and planning procedures put on a more reliable scientific basis. Rather belatedly it has been discovered that in conditions of industrial maturity we need to choose hitherto untried methods. We lack experience, and therefore we shall probably have to pay a certain price for them. The main thing is that it should be kept to a minimum. Any help afforded by a growth theory that proved suitable for application in practice would consequently be expected to meet with a welcome from the central planners.

However, specificity is a somewhat relative term. There are many common features, especially among the industrially advanced socialist countries, all of which are in large measure dependent on foreign trade. This gives the authors cause to hope that their work will contribute to the general discussion among socialist economists on questions of growth and the functioning of a socialist economy.

Although we are concerned with an introduction to a subject that is comparatively little known in Czechoslovak literature, some results of original research are included. This applies, for instance, to the relation between model factors ("model" in respect of the model of operation of a socialist economy) and structural factors at work during acceleration or deceleration of growth. Similarly, analysis of preceding development from the standpoint of growth theory, in other words application of the growth model to empirical data for 1950−65, covers almost untouched ground.

The book draws on studies of various aspects, published in Czechoslovakia and other countries during recent years. The days are past when an economist was wont to write a big book from scratch and then present it for his readers to judge. A more fruitful approach would seem to be the method that has been adopted especially among western scholars, whereby the more bulky volumes are not published until the results of partial studies have stood the test of constructive criticism that is bound to enrich every such work. The articles that form one of the main elements in this publication have appeared in a number of countries; reprints (or comprehensive excerpts) have been published in Norway, Poland, Italy, Hungary, the US, Yugoslavia, France and the USSR.[1] They were followed by a fairly wide discussion in Poland and in Czechoslovakia. Since these contributions were favourably received both in socialist and capitalist countries, we may venture to hope that this book, too, will play a part in developing a dialogue between economists in the West and East.

We should emphasise at the start that not all the ideas can be precisely accredited to their authors. Indeed, probably in no other branch of learning

[1] *Economics of Planning*, Oslo, vol. 4, 1964, vol. 6, 1966, no. 2, *Życie Gospodarcze*, 1965, no. 7, p. 2, *Gospodarka planowa*, 1965, no. 4, pp. 49−56, 1965, no. 5, pp. 47−49; *Polityka*, Warsaw, 1965, nos. 4 and 5; *Rinascita*, Jan. 16, 1965, pp. 20−1; *Közgazdasági Szemle*, 1965, no. 9, pp. 1132−9; *Eastern European Economics*, New York, vol. IV., 1965, no. 1; *Zbornik Radova Čehoslovačkih ekonomista*, Belgrade, 1965, pp. 240−261, 284−301; *La revue L'U.R.S.S. et les pays de l'Est*, 1965, no. 3; *Problèmes Economiques*, Dec. 7, 1965; *Mirovaya ekonomika i mezhdunarodnie otnosheniya*, 1966, no. 2; *Życie Gospodarcze*, 1966, no. 13, p. 8.

is the ancient principle of Roman law, *pater semper incertus*, so apt. The indispensability of comparative studies when analysing complex processes of economic events and the consequent need to know some of the specific conditions of individual countries, and finally the absolute necessity of linking a synthetic approach at a national-economic level with investigation on the lines of sectoral economics, all this makes it impossible for a useful analysis to appear from the pen of an individual. Far behind us are the days, although their echoes are sometimes apt to linger in our minds, when the *Privat-Gelehrter* could sit quietly and alone in his study and produce an interesting work. Right at the start of empirical economic research in the post-war Czechoslovak Republic it was discovered that the only fruitful method of work in this field was team work (*Plánované hospodářství v ČSR* by J. Goldmann, J. Flek, Orbis 1948, pp. 10−11), and this is a hundred times more true today. Our knowledge of the economic processes has been extended, and the complexity of economic events has grown considerably. The sooner we get rid of the relics of craft methods still surviving in the economic work of some of our institutions, the better for authors and for the progress of our economic science.

Last but not least, we wish to thank all those who in many consultations and discussions have with complete unselfishness devoted so much of their time to making this work better than it could have been if such contact with economists in Czechoslovakia and elsewhere had been lacking.

On some specific matters, the authors consulted J. Flek, L. Hejl, L. Jüngling, M. Kadlec, B. Levčík, V. Nachtigal, O. Šik, J. Toman and Z. Vergner. M. Kalecki and W. Brus (Warsaw) have provided valuable impulses to the writing of the book and their help in clarifying its concept has been of great significance. Other economists who have advised on selected questions include I. Friss (Budapest), G. Kohlmey (Berlin), R. Krengel (West Berlin), K. Laski, A. Lukaszewicz (Warsaw), and others. In expressing their thanks for the help received, the authors accept sole responsibility for any shortcomings and errors.

Thanks are also due to K. Janáček and J. Rybáčková for assistance to the authors.

Prague, May 1966.

# Contents

Chapter I

# Theory of Economic Growth

"A science that does not examine its own history cannot claim to be called a science".

KARL MARX

## a) Origin and social background

The theory of economic growth is a very young science, the origins of which are to be found in the works of some western authors. The causes of its origin lie in the socio-economic conditions of the inter-war period and in changes occurring after World War II.

The depression of the thirties shook the foundations of the capitalist system and, in face of coexistence with the socialist sixth of the world, the very existence of capitalism was in question. This evoked the social demand for a new theory that would not explain a fictitious, non-existent equilibrium, but the actual, highly dramatic cyclical course of the reproduction process. This order placed by society was met after a stubborn fight between the old and new schools of social economics in the course of the "Keynesian revolution". The theory of the conjunctural cycle, whose main proponents were J. M. Keynes and M. Kalecki, set out to elucidate the causes of cyclical changes in the capitalist economy and attempted to determine the reasons for crisis and unemployment.

Contemporary growth theory ties up with the theory of the conjunctural cycle and may be regarded as a critical development of Keynes' line of thought. While Keynes was concerned with the causes of cyclical development, that is with short-term changes in the growth rate, the new discipline examines the factors determining and guaranteeing the long-term growth rate. In the post-war economic and social situation a conjunctural, anti-cyclical policy alone was not enough to achieve stable economic growth, it was necessary to engage in theoretical investigation of the mechanism of long-term movements in the capitalist economy. And such research was not actuated solely by the internal needs of capitalism; a big influence was exerted by the changes engendered through the emergence of the world socialist system, and by the struggle with the "third world".

The founders of the present theory of economic growth may be taken to be R. F. Harrod and E. D. Domar, while leading names in this field are those of M. Kalecki, N. Kaldor and Joan Robinson, together with R. M. Solow and J. E. Meade. Harrod and Domar are concerned with growth of the economy as a whole. They have worked out a one-sector model that is applicable, after modification, to a socialist economy. The Harrod-Domar model was the first attempt to dynamise the Keynesian economic macro-analysis. It is among the most valuable contributions and starting points for contemporary growth theory.[1] Domar's ideas on amortization and renewal in the process of growth are also significant. He is among those non-Marxist economists who give serious attention to Marxist economics and place high value on some of its works, especially the pioneering growth model constructed by the Soviet economist, G. A. Feldman, in 1928.

Modern growth theory has many points of contact with the works of Adam Smith, David Ricardo and especially Karl Marx. Marx's analysis of the reproduction process elucidates some of the fundamental relationships among elements of macroeconomic nature. In examining the interdependence of capital, employment, demand, production of consumer goods and investment trends, he deals with processes that are known in contemporary growth theory as the multiplier and acceleration effects. His theoretical presentation of the reproduction process embodies a dynamic view of the economy and differs sharply from the stationary concept that was imported for a time into economic theory by the Austrian school. A certain affinity between growth theory and Marx's ideas has, indeed, been pointed out by Domar; growth models in the wider sense have often appeared in economic writings, starting, in his opinion, at least from Marx. He believes that the Marxists have of all economic schools come closest to a fundamental growth theory and that their successes could be greater if they spent less time and

---

[1]  In Western economics, we often meet with two concepts, Economic Development, and Economic Growth. Insofar as they are not taken to be synonymous, the former usually denotes both the quantitative relationships among growth factors and the overall economic, social, i.e. including institutional, changes that are determined by economic growth and react upon it.

energy commenting the works of their master. Some excellently worked out and interesting models have appeared in Soviet writings.[2]

In this connection it is in place to stress the significant role played by M. Kalecki in developing the growth theory of capitalism. We may quote the view of one of the leading western econometrists, L. R. Klein: "The econometric models that I have constructed as practical tools for analyzing or predicting the economies of the United States, Canada, United Kingdom, and Japan have been based on combinations from the theoretical models of Marx, Kalecki, Keynes, Lange, Hicks, Kaldor, Metzler, Goodwin, and others. It is fitting at this time to re-examine the position of the Kalecki model in this hierarchy and its relevance to model building of the present day.

The Marxian schemes of reproduction and accumulation and the Keynesian models of effective demand are the forerunners of the present theoretical model building. It is often not adequately appreciated how the Kalecki model, constructed in the Marxian spirit, actually pre-shadowed all the essential ingredients of the Keynesian system that have made the latter system so popular among the present generation of Western economists. It is usually thought that the recent rapid development of macroeconomic model building in the econometric branch of the subject is an outgrowth of the neo-Keynesian development. Actually most models in existence today could be decomposed into ideas first found in the models of Kalecki, Kaldor, Metzler, and Goodwin. The latter three could have been developed as natural extensions of the Kalecki theory. The mathematical interpretations of Keynes by Lange and Hicks undoubtedly reinforced the development and certainly enhanced it, but the basic ingredients of the Keynesian development were already available in Kalecki's model."[3]

A certain analogy may be said to exist between the development of growth theory under capitalism and under socialism. Just as bourgeois development theory was in many ways the apologetics for capitalism and only became a science after the crisis of the thirties, the theory of expanded socialist reproduction was in the traditional concept of the personality cult phase to a large extent the pseudo-scientific apologetics for economic reality

[2]  E. D. DOMAR, *Essays in the Theory of Economic Growth*, New York 1957.

[3]  L. R. KLEIN, *Role of Econometrics in Socialist Economics*, Problems of Economic Dynamics and Planning, Warsaw 1964, p. 189.

at any price, with all its shortcomings, and an uncritical defence of the dogmatic approach to economic growth. The outcome of this deformation in the sphere of economic theory and the management of the national economy was the unsatisfactory reality of socialist economic development in recent times, which contrasted so sharply with the actual growth potential. The deterioration in the economic situation that set in in the early sixties, combined with the social regeneration evoked by the Twentieth Congress of the Soviet Communist Party, opened the door to a gradual renaissance of Marxist thinking.

In the traditional form accorded to it in the days when dogmatic thinking held the field, the theory of reproduction revolved around the interpretation of Marx's equilibrium formulae. In the early fifties, discussion was still confined to the argument − largely sterile − whether Marx's reproduction formulae with its symbols could be used at all to depict equilibrium conditions under socialism. Finally, in 1952, Stalin in his *Economic Problems of Socialism in the USSR* "settled" the argument by pointing to a note in which Lenin, discussing Bukharin's book, said that the formula $1(v + m) = IIc$ would be valid even under communism. Any consideration of growth factors dropped out of the field of study and on the level of economic policies its place was taken by the *a priori* insistence on maximum production rates, with Department I outpacing Department II.

Only under the pressure of the problems facing the socialist economy − one might say *ex post facto* − did research proceed to examine the question of economic growth rates and the interplay of growth factors. This extended the field of issues that were not the direct subject of Marx's work and for a long time − with rare exceptions in the late twenties − were not touched by Marxist economists at all.

Study of economic processes under socialist conditions is still at a stage where the white patches on the map of our knowledge are only gradually being filled in. With increasing clarity it is being found that the reproduction process in a socialist economy cannot be fully elucidated and its laws cannot be discerned so long as the method employed is at bottom confined to dogmatic paraphrasing and harping on Marx's formulae.

Evidently any creative development of the theory of socialist expanded reproduction will take in, step by step, research on the interplay of growth factors and the progress of socialist production relations conditioned by them. That is to say, the acutal subject matter of a socialist growth theory are the interrelationships — causal and functional — among the different growth factors in the context of a given form of socialist production relations, i.e. in the framework of a given model of the operation of a socialist economy.

It now remains to define the connection between the theory of economic growth under socialism and the theory of socialist reproduction. In the terminology used by Polish authors, the theory of socialist reproduction embraces both the study of economic growth, which deals with growth processes only in physical terms, and the question of equilibrium, i.e. the value aspect in terms of money.

In analysing the direct factors, growth theory examines the influence of employment and labour productivity on the growth rate of the national income. Indirect factors are taken to be investment and the effectiveness of capital assets. Theoretical analysis shows the correlation of these growth factors, especially the influence of production relations on individual growth factors, while also studying the barriers to growth (consumption, employment, the material barrier and foreign trade).

The interrelationships of growth factors are usually formalized by means of mathematical models. In an empirico-statistically oriented analysis of the growth process, verification is then carried out with the help of statistical data. Theoretical works in the field of economic growth serve as instruments in analysing development, as a source of scientific information for policy-making, while also giving guidance and instruments for long-term projections in planning work.

## b) Economic discussion of the twenties: G. A. Feldman's model

Undoubtedly all Marxist economists who are concerned with the theory of growth — and non-Marxists like Domar — feel an obligation to pay tribute to the proud memory of those who nearly half a century ago laid the foundations for a splendid construction of economic growth theory under socialism and for a genuinely scientific method of socialist planning. It was not their fault, but — to use the customary terminology — a result of the personality cult, that on these foundations there arose throughout the Stalinist world — to the grave detriment of the socialist cause — the structure of a quite different branch of science. This is the discipline that for many years adorned the political economy text-books under the undeserved title "Theory of Socialist Expanded Reproduction"[4].

The second half of the twenties was notable for fruitful work on compiling long-term, general plans. As soon as NEP had fulfilled its first aim, and postwar reconstruction had been successfully completed, the question arose of what next — the question of the start and trajectory of economic growth.

General plans were worked out for periods of 10 – 15 years. Their aim was to achieve structural changes in the economy, raise living standards as quickly as possible, and win a leading place in world economy. The precondition was to master the methods and technique of planning for growth. In working on the plans, Soviet experts tackled the problem of finding, within the existing economic structure, a possible transition to a new structure. In so doing, they were, in fact, considering questions of dynamic equilibrium-questions that are connected with the theory of economic growth.

The drafts of general plans for socialist construction envisaged building up socialism in the USSR within 10 to 15 years; some foresaw the possibility of catching up with the United States in all basic indicators — including living standards — within 12 to 14 years.

The method of compiling these plans was very interesting. Work was delegated to various institutions, groups of authors, and to individuals. This resulted in several variants, of which the optimal was chosen. Moreover, the discussions of the twenties are notable for the amazingly diverse and many-sided problems tackled. The plans were debated in Gosplan, in the Conjunctural Institute, the Council of Labour and Defence, the Central Statistical Office and elsewhere. Discussion was conducted in the columns of journals devoted almost entirely to economic problems, while features were the strong participation by executives in the economic field, and the high theoretical level.

---

[4] In this connection one can only express regret that a serious study on the subject "Economic consequences of dogmatism in the political economy of socialism" has been waiting so long for its authors.

During preparation of the "genplans", G. A. Feldman was entrusted with working out a model of long-term growth. In this model, constructed in 1928, the author attempted to define the conditions for optimalization of the growth process, taken in the context of a given set of preconditions and interrelationships. He formulated a number of linkages among growth factors; their rediscovery in the forties by E. D. Domar, originator of modern growth theory in the West, is of relevance for the socialist countries, too.

Feldman made the first attempt in the history of economics to advance a theory of growth for socialism. He investigated the correlations between accumulation and consumption, trends of wages and productivity, personal and social consumption, at varying rates of growth of the national income. His theory also included an attempt to solve the problem of retardation and acceleration of growth, i.e. the problem of the conditions and substance of changes in the growth rate in time, and with productive equipment of varying efficiency. In addition to its historical value, Feldman's model contains conclusions that are quite topical even today. Moreover, since he raises a number of interesting questions, his approach and results deserve further development and confrontation with the present stage of research and with discussions in this field.

The immediate subject of Feldman's work was Soviet economic growth, its existing state and underlying conditions, and the future outlook. The one and only socialist economy of the day was functioning in an economically backward country at the threshold of its stormy and epic advance up to the level of the most developed countries in the world. Moreover, this path was to be accompanied by massive transformations, structural, economic and social. In view of the analogies to be observed in the world today, this circumstance is an added reason for taking notice of Feldman's work.

He published his ideas in a fairly short article in the journal *Planovoye Khozyaystvo*.[5] He was on the staff of the Soviet Gosplan at the time and was engaged in work intended to be preparatory to the first Soviet economic plan to cover a period of some years. For the young planned economy, the first in the world, this was a turning point, a time of transition from not

---

[5] See A. LUKASZEWICZ, *Przyspieszony wzrost gospodarki socjalistycznej w związku z teorie G. Feldmana*, Warsaw 1965; J. CHLUMSKÝ, "Feldmanova a Harrodova-Domarova teorie růstu", *Politická ekonomie*, no. 11/1965.

very precise annual plans, i.e. based on "check figures", to more elaborated and detailed five-year plans. In those days Soviet planners conceived the idea of embarking on the bold and far-sighted project of planning for a period of twenty or more years. Working in this environment, Feldman made the immediate aim of the research referred to above the endeavour to formulate a theoretical basis for such a planning method. This gave his theory two features, in that it attempted to formulate both the general theoretical foundations of long-term planning, and a theory of economic growth in a socialist planned economy.

To define the goal, that is to determine the possible dimensions of consumption and the growth rate in relation to the structure of the national economy, is highly topical, since it continues to be the central problem in Marxist growth theory and in the theory and practice of planning.

Feldman proposed a draft plan in the form of a system of indicators, which he defined in formulae. And he saw this model — the plan in abstract — as the base for elaborating the perspective development plan to whatever degree of detail and concrete targets might be desired. In many clear-cut ideas he went far beyond his times.[6]

6 "What form should the overall economic plan take? We assume that the plan may be brought to whatever degree of detail and concreteness that is desired, but the draft of the plan (taking the plan to be not just a model, but a perspective plan of development), the plan in its abstract form, must in all events and primarily be composed of a *system* comprising a set of the indicators given in our formulae.

The system of formulae and the method of analysis proposed by us may appear to be too complicated and difficult to manage. We consider it necessary to protest at the start most emphatically against such a view. It is impossible to imagine a *simple* method for designing such a *complicated apparatus* as the national economy. On the other hand, we know of no better form of analysis than mathematics. Anyone acquainted with the theories of various machines will hardly be likely to contend that our method is more complicated than that created by the theory of hydraulic turbines or electrical machines. For instance, A. Pfarr's theory of hydro-turbines occupies 821 pages, the theory of direct-current generators is expounded on 816 pages by E. Arnold, and the entire theory of electrical machines takes up several such volumes. By the size of these works one can get some idea of the intricacy and detail of the theoretical treatment. One can find everything in these works — from the most general formulae to the concrete expression of all details. They are based on the laws of physics and mathematics, which did not, however, exclude the

Feldman's importance for socialist economics derives from one more circumstance. Up to the fifties his theory provided the only developed model of economic growth under socialism. Much of the work dating from those days concerning the theory of reproduction, or growth and equilibrium in a capitalist economy, was simply an elaboration of Marx's theory of capitalist reproduction, or related to discussions carried on by Lenin, Rosa Luxemburg and Otto Bauer. The treatment of the theoretical aspects of socialist reproduction was at that time merely introductory and more or less chance.

The Soviet discussion of the early thirties on the so-called dampening curve was conducted at a level of purely empirical economic policy, or on a historical-comparative level of statistics.

Several circumstances contributed to the fact that Feldman (in common with other Soviet economists of the day, but Feldman particularly, in view of the significance of his theoretical contribution) was ahead of his times. The circumstances under which his theory came to be forgotten were largely of a passing political nature. Its fate, which was in no way exceptional, could provide a rewarding subject for study by sociologists of science.

Feldman's work gives a genuinely developed Marxist theory of economic growth. Although his treatment may seem to us today overcomplicated in some respects, its substance is modern and still largely relevant.

---

formulation of a concrete theory of constructing the machines used in production...

... We are convinced that more or less perfect planning of the national economy can be achieved only on the basis of a theory formulated in precise mathematical terms. Only then can disputes about plans be brought to the point of fundamental directives and targets, with full certainty that the calculations are correct. Hitherto unmanageable spontaneous factors will be determined solely by choosing definite variants, prepared beforehand as in plans of combat. Moreover, it should be stressed that planning the national economy for the coming year can be considered purely as a concretisation of the first sector of a plan for economic development covering many years."

G. A. FELDMAN, "K teorii temp narodnogo dokhoda", *Planovoye Khozyaystvo*, nos. 11 and 12/1928, pp. 177—8.

Chapter II

# Kalecki's Growth Model

"... to make a scientific plan for such a developing socio-economic and technical entity as the Soviet land is to become over the next five to ten years is in fact unthinkable without a corresponding scientific method. If the genius of antique builders enabled them to build splendid buildings, although they probably lacked even a fraction of the scientific knowledge that is expected of a modern builder, who aspires to the right to build quite simple constructions and machines, this does not imply that in building our economy we should and can be guided by the example of ancient times. We do not know what number of buildings were never completed or how many came to an untimely end just because the builders' intuition could not compensate for a lack of scientific method... We cannot and may not allow ourselves the luxury of employing in our economy an unsuccessful project, an unsuccessful variant. From this follows the absolute necessity of a scientific apparatus and scientific method. While knowledge of Marx's general laws is certainly necessary, it is not an adequate equipment. The need for a logical system of formulae defining the necessary dynamic relationships among the basic elements of the national economy seems to us obvious. With the complexity of the tasks facing us, it is clear that use of this system of formulae calls for the method of 'progressive approximation'. Experience of various projects goes to prove it. But without theory, the method of 'progressive approximation' turns either into a prophecy or into the Sisyphean labour of a constructeur of genius, who substitutes intuition for method and system."

G. A. FELDMAN, 1928

## a)  Brief account of Kalecki's growth model

Kalecki's model of the growth of a socialist economy, which was presented in outline at the second congress of Polish economists in 1956, played a key part in theoretical discussions in Poland, in research on the fundamental processes in a socialist economy, and in constructing the first variants of the long-term plan for the People's Republic of Poland up to 1975. The model has been improved and amplified several times, culminating in the systematic account given in *Zarys teorii vzrostu gospodarki socjalistycznej*, published in Warsaw in 1963 (and in 1965 in Czech translation in Prague).

The starting point of Kalecki's work is the view that analysis of the functional relationships embodied in the model is impossible if the *basic factors* — the production relations — are not taken into consideration. Behind the apparently slight divergences between the model formulated by Kalecki for analysing the growth factors of socialism and some of the models known in the West, there lies in reality a fundamental difference. This emerges when the formal correlations are subjected to analysis from the standpoint of the conditions and assumptions stemming from the social order. That is to say, the production relations (or institutional factors) determine the nodal parameters of every model representing quantitative correlations among growth factors.

In stressing the superiority of a planned socialist economy with regard to the opportunities of utilizing the social potential of growth, Kalecki firmly rejects voluntarism in planning the growth rate, especially in setting an overhigh rate of investment. Hence the role played in this theory by analysis of growth barriers, which, if ignored, would induce a reduction in long-term growth rate compared with the original intentions. From this standpoint, too, he emphasizes the need to respect the development of consumption in the short term. He demonstrates that non-adherence to this principle induces negative effects both socially and in the purely economic field — through the bad echo-effect on labour productivity.

The special attention that Kalecki devotes to growth barriers in no way leads him to a fatalistic conclusion as to the inevitability of accommodating to the given constraining factors. On the contrary, he underlines the importance of looking for effective means of overcoming them through increasing the efficiency of the economic process.

Kalecki's growth model expresses the correlations of individual growth factors and increment in the national income, i.e. the growth rate. The national income, denoted by the symbol $D$, is taken to be the total output in a given year, excluding the value of raw materials produced and semifabricates consumed in the production process. But we do not deduct from the value of output the value of capital assets consumed, i.e. amortization. In Kalecki's model we are therefore working with the gross national income. If $I$ denotes investment in production (gross), $O$ the increment of circulating assets and $S$ consumption in the broad sense (personal and social, and nonproductive investment), we have the following equation:

$$D = I + O + S \qquad (1)$$

where $I + O$ is the total production accumulation (with production investment as a gross figure, including amortization).

Increment in the national income, denoted as $\Delta D$, is the product of
production investments put into operation during the year. The input of
capital goods per unit increase in the national income will be termed the
marginal capital-output ratio, denoted by the symbol $m$.

The relation between addition to the national income and production
investment can then be expressed

$$\Delta D = \frac{I}{m} \qquad (2)$$

where $m = I/\Delta D$

Other factors beside investment influence increase in the national income. They include primarily obsolescence of production equipment. The
scrapping of production assets reduces capacity with a consequent drop in
the formation of national income by $aD$, where $a$ is the coefficient of amortization. This item expresses decline in the national income due to cuts in
the production apparatus brought about by eliminating capital assets from
the reproduction process. Taking this factor into account, we get the
equation:

$$\Delta D = \frac{I}{m} - aD \qquad (3)$$

A source of increase in the national income also lies in improvements
independent of investment in production. These non-investment sources
stem from improvements in organization of work, savings of raw materials,
reduction of waste etc. The national income shows an annual growth from
this source of $uD$, where the $u$-factor is the coefficient of improvements
leading with existing equipment to higher output.

Expanded to include the $u$-factor, the equation is:

$$\Delta D = \frac{I}{m} - aD + uD \qquad (4)$$

23

Dividing both sides of the equation by the national income $D$, we get for the growth rate of the national income $r = \Delta D/D$:

$$r = \frac{1}{m}\frac{I}{D} - a + u \tag{5}$$

This formula is known as Kalecki's growth model; it depicts the chief correlations to be met with in the process of economic growth.

This basic formula can be expanded to give full expression to the influence of productive accumulation, including increments in circulating assets, on the growth rate of the national income. Actually we have for the meantime taken into consideration solely one component of productive accumulation, i.e. additions to the fixed production assets. But growth in national income is also influenced by the second component i.e. additions to circulating assets, in which Kalecki includes any rise or fall in the volume of construction-in-progress.

For simplicity, he assumes that with a given commodity structure, circulating assets grow in proportion to the national income. Therefore their increment is proportional to increment in the national income. In this case, the correlation between growth of circulating assets and that of the national income may be expressed as follows:

$$O = \mu\,\Delta D \tag{6}$$

where $Q$, as mentioned above, is the addition to circulating assets (including the volume of construction-in-progress) and $\mu$ is the relation of the level of circulating assets to the national income, in other words, the so-called average inventory turnover period.

Using equations (5) and (6) we can express the correlation between the growth rate of the national income and the share of productive accumulation in the national income. Equation (5) may be written:

$$\frac{I}{D} = (r + a - u)\,m$$

and equation (6) can be written:

$$\frac{O}{D} = \mu\,\frac{\Delta D}{D} = \mu r$$

By combining the two equations we get:

$$\frac{I + O}{D} = (m + \mu)\,r + (a - u)\,m$$

and hence by a simple adjustment:

$$r = \frac{1}{m + \mu} \cdot \frac{I + O}{D} = \frac{m}{m + \mu}(a - u) \tag{7}$$

Since total production accumulation is given by the sum $I + O$, its share in the national income, denoted by $i$, may be expressed as follows:

$$i = \frac{I + O}{D}$$

Further, we may denote the sum $m + \mu$ by the symbol $k$. This quantity tells us the amount of investment and circulating assets necessary to obtain a unit increment in national income. We will term it the average capital-output ratio. After introducing the quantities $i$ and $k$ into equation (7), we get:

$$r = \frac{i}{k} - \frac{m}{k}(a - u) \tag{8}$$

For illustration let us assume that $i = 24\%$; $k = 4$; $m = 2$; $a = 2\%$; $u = 3\%$. In this case, the growth rate of the national income will be 6·5%, because

$$r = \frac{24}{4} - \frac{2}{4}(2 - 3) = 6{\cdot}5$$

Kalecki's growth model enables long-term changes in the national income and its components to be studied. If $k$ and $m$ are constants, and assuming there is no change in the $a$-factor or the $u$-factor, maintenance of constant growth requires a constant share of productive accumulation in the national income. This signifies that with a constant growth rate, net capital formation grows at the same rate as the national income. Since the share of consumption in the national income $(1 - i)$ is dependent on the trend of the share of productive accumulation, consumption and accumulation grow, under the condition we have assumed, at the same rate as the national income. From the standpoint of the relation between production of means of production (Department I) and production of articles of consumption (Department II), this implies that on the above assumptions, Departments I and II should develop at an equal rate.

The situation is different with accelerated growth. With $k$, $m$, $a$ and $u$ unchanged, the growth rate of the national income can be speeded up only by raising the share of productive accumulation. Since the latter consists physically of products of Department I, accelerated growth under our conditions is accompanied by a higher growth rate of Department I compared with Department II. In this case, however, accelerated growth will involve a fall in the share of consumption in the national income. The higher the growth rate of the national income $r$, the higher the share of production accumulation $i$ in the national income, and the lower the share of consumption $(1 - i)$.

Under certain circumstances, we meet with growth in the share of productive accumulation and priority growth of Department I over Department II even in cases where the need for accelerated growth does not arise. If with constant $a$- and $u$-factors, the average capital-output ratio moves upward, a constant rate can only be maintained through a growing share of productive accumulation, and hence more rapid growth of Department I. The trend of the capital-output ratio is affected by two factors. The first is the character of technological development, the second may lie in structural changes.

We are witnesses of three types of technological advance:

1.  technological advance with a rising capital-output ratio (rising $k$-factor);
2.  technological advance with a sinking capital-output ratio (sinking $k$-factor);
3.  a neutral type (constant $k$-factor).

Dependent on the movement of the $k$-factor, in order to maintain a given rate — with other circumstances equal — it is necessary to choose a rising, sinking or constant accumulation rate, and hence relationship between Departments I and II.

This brief indication of the leading correlations and their projection in Kalecki's model already opens the door to resolving the puzzle of Departments I and II and breaks the seal of secret and inviolable dogma imposed by the Stalin period of economic thinking. From our brief account of the basic relationships it follows that priority growth of Department I is not essential for expanded reproduction.[1]

With a growing rate of accumulation, and with it priority growth of Department I, we meet in effect in cases where there is accelerated growth with an unchanged capital-output ratio or maintenance of a given growth rate with a rising capital-output ratio.

Correlation between the marginal capital-output ratio and the overall industrial structure was already noted by G. Feldman, "For different production sectors the $C$ coefficients (i.e., in effect the marginal capital-output ratios − our note) are different, and with a change in the structure of production, changes in the share of individual production sectors in overall production alter the $C$ coefficient, too, for the national economy as a whole. From this also stems the great significance of structural changes for the value expression of overall production."[2]

Regarding the long-term dynamics of the capital-output ratio there are three groups of opinion:

1.  The capital-output ratio is constant.[3]

2.  The capital-output ratio is a constantly shrinking quantity.[4]

---

[1]  Compare the concept that so long dominated economic theory and practice − "Priority growth in production of means of production is essential not only because its output has to equip both its own enterprises and those of the other sectors of the national economy, but also because without it it is absolutely impossible to achieve extended reproduction." J. V. STALIN, *Economic Problems of Socialism*.

[2]  G. A. FELDMAN, ibid. no. 12, p. 175.

[3]  See R. HARROD, *Towards a Dynamic Economics*, 1948; E. DOMAR, *Essays in the Theory of Economic Growth*, New York 1957; W. LEONTIEV and others, *Issledovaniya struktury amerikanskoy ekonomiki*, Moscow 1959; R. SOLOW, "Technical Change and Aggregate Production Function", *Review of Economics and Statistics* 1957, vol. XXXIX; J. TINBERGEN, H. BOS, *Mathematical Models of Economic Growth*, New York 1962, p. 37.

[4]  See R. GOLDSMITH, *The National Wealth of the United States in the Postwar Period*, Princeton 1962; TH. VAN DER WEIDE, *Statistics of National Wealth for 18 Countries, Income and Wealth Series* 1969, vol. VIII.

3.    In the initial and middle stages of industrialization the capital-output ratio rises, then remains constant for a time, followed by a downward move.[5]

Data from the advanced capitalist countries do not confirm the view that contemporary developments in science and technology induce a rise in capital inputs (Table 1). The table gives the marginal capital-output ratio (in our terminology, sometimes also the coefficient of demand on assets) which expresses the relationship of total capital production assets to the national income. The recent fall in this ratio implies an even greater drop in the (incremental) coefficient of demand on capital. There can be no question of any lasting upward movement in either coefficient for the countries concerned. The western expert in this field, Prof. S. Kuznets, mentions in his last work on postwar economic growth[6] that the ratio of capital to production has fallen over the past 150 years by one-fifth; he based this on data from a number of advanced capitalist countries.

The insistence that growth of capital inputs is essential is a dogma that obscures the true possibilities of economic development. Evidently the reason for clinging to the dogma lies in the fact that the specific conditions of socialist industrialisation in the Soviet Union (and in Czechoslovakia), when primarily in connection with a shift to sectors making heavy claims on assets, the capital-output ratio rose, were given such absolute validity that they are now considered as applicable even in the present quite disparate situation.

The rate of investment input has a fundamental influence on the development of the rate of net capital formation, which is why the rigid classical approach arrives at the supposedly essential growth in the share of accumulation. The formulation of such a "law" at the existing level of economic theory and with the empirical data available today simply shows how long-drawn and difficult is the struggle of the old with the new in the thinking of us all.

---

[5]    See S. KUZNETS, *Capital in the American Economy. Its Formation and Financing*, New York 1962; C. CLARK, *Conditions of Economic Progress*, 3rd edition, London 1957, pp. 503, 569; R. BICANIC, "Threshold of Economic Growth", *Kyklos* 1962, vol. XV, no. 1.

[6]    Cambridge, Mass 1964.

**Table 1.** *Dynamics of the capital-output ratio in the USA and West Germany*

| USA | | GFR | |
|---|---|---|---|
| Year | Capital-output ratio | Year | Capital-output ratio |
| 1896—1901 | 3·04 | 1897—1900 | 2·86 |
| 1902—1907 | 2·78 | 1904—1907 | 2·97 |
| 1908—1913 | 2·91 | 1910—1913 | 3·22 |
| 1925—1930 | 3·16 | 1927—1929 | 2·87 |
| 1931—1936 | 3·69 | 1937—1938 | 3·11 |
| 1937—1941 | 3·01 | 1955—1957 | 2·87 |
| 1953—1958 | 2·26 | | |

Source: B. N. MIKHALEVSKI, *Perspektivnye raschoty na osnove prostykh dina-micheskikh modeley*, Moscow 1964, pp. 41, 42. *Trends in the American Economy in the Nineteenth Century*, p. 39.

Under present conditions the typical trend is for the capital-output ratio to remain steady or even to sink. Nor is continuously accelerating growth an objectively given long-term tendency (indeed, continuously high growth rates are not even possible). Consequently, the "economic law" of gradual increase in the share of accumulation in the national income is artificial, as empirically demonstrated by the data in Table 2.

**Table 2.** *Trend of the rate of net capital formation in Great Britain and the USA*

| Great Britain | | USA | |
|---|---|---|---|
| Year | Rate | Year | Rate |
| 1870—1899 | 11·0 | 1869—1898 | 13·5 |
| 1880—1913 | 11·9 | 1899—1928 | 12·7 |
| 1950—1955 | 7·2 | 1919—1948 | 8·7 |
| | | 1950—1955 | 11·1 |

Source: S. KUZNETS, *Six Lectures on Economic Growth*, New York 1961, pp. 82 and 83. (On page 84 the author writes, on the basis of an analysis of data for a larger number of countries, that most show a sinking rate of net capital formation in the long term).

The initial economic backwardness of most socialist countries and the need for an accelerated process of industrialization was reflected in economic theory by strong underlining of growth rates and raising the share of net capital formation. The social-economic conditions of socialism do not restrain the growth rate by the limits of effective demand and enable the principle of rational performance to be applied on the macroeconomic scale. But this does not imply that the approach to choice of a growth rate is easy or that the potentialities offered by the new social order have always been used to the best purpose. In the economic theory and practice of some socialist countries, including Czechoslovakia, there have been times when an above-optimum rate has been chosen and the barriers of economic growth have been ignored.

A high growth rate is not an end in itself. Under normal circumstances, the chief criterion in choosing the rate is the growth of consumption, both in the short and long term.[7]

While the process of economic growth at a given steady rate does not normally involve complications, a transition to accelerated growth induces various difficulties and may come up against growth barriers.

The prime barrier to growth that has to be respected insofar as extra-economic considerations are not given priority in choosing, is that of consumption. The transition to a rising share of net capital formation in production has its limits, because it simultaneously signifies a corresponding cut in the share of consumption. "This relative reduction in consumption for the immediate future is a sacrifice that we make in order to speed up the growth rate of the national income and consequently of consumption, too, in the long term, which is favourably influenced by a cumulatively increasing rate of growth of the national income. Decisions concerning the choice of the magnitude of $r$ will therefore be a compromise between the negative

---

[7] See G. A. Feldman: "Since consumption is in fact the goal of production, growth in consumption should interest us above all when we speak of the national income. Productive accumulation should interest us primarily as a means towards raising consumption and the rate of its growth. From this standpoint the only rival to consumption can be the need to strengthen the country's defence ..." G. A. FELDMAN, ibid. no. 11, p. 150.

effect of a higher growth rate for the immediate future and the positive effect in the more distant future."[8]

Full employment also exerts a strong restraint on choice of a higher growth rate that would be threatened by the manpower barrier. With a manpower shortage, a higher growth rate can be aimed at only to the extent that investment leads to savings in living labour. If this condition is not met, there is no point in stepping up the share of net capital formation in the national income, because this would lead to building unused production capacities. A special type of manpower barrier is a labour force with an unsuitable composition of skills, especially in developing countries suffering from shortages of skilled personnel.

There may also be an organizational barrier to accelerated growth, because more widespread investment makes greater claims on organizational and designing preparation, on smooth deliveries, cooperation etc.

Accelerated economic growth may be considerably complicated by a material barrier, which is usually intimately linked with the foreign trade barrier. Growing demand for raw materials makes increasing claims on import, and hence on bigger exports to cover the gap in a strained trade balance. Growing export as a rule meets with difficulties in placing goods on foreign markets. The drive to export at any cost evokes a deterioration in the terms of trade. Similar effects follow from a transition to markets with less advantageous price relations and the inclusion of less profitable commodities among export items. Growing tension in the trade balance generates an endeavour to restrict imports, encouraging autarchic tendencies evinced in higher production costs. In these circumstances, there will be a trend towards rising investment and labour inputs per unit of national income.

The choice of a growth rate is among the most complicated problems of economic theory and one of the most responsible issues in planning and economic policy.[9] The guarantee of advance is not a maximum growth rate,

---

[8]  M. KALECKI, *Zarys teorii wzrostu gospodarki socjalistycznej*, Warsaw 1963, p. 35.

[9]  For a more detailed account of Kalecki's growth model see *Ekonomia polityczna socjalizmu*, edited by W. BRUS, Warsaw 1964, K. LASKI, *Zarys teorii reprodukcji socjalistycznej*, Warsaw 1965. For the relationship between Departments I and II see also O. LANGE, *Teoria reprodukcji i akumulacji*, Warsaw 1961, chapter II., or K. KOUBA et al., *Politická ekonomie socialismu*, Prague 1964.

but an optimal rate leading to stable, balanced growth, without harmful fluctuations.

Examination of growth factors also indicates that the growth rate does not depend exclusively on the development of the capital-output ratio and the level of net capital formation. Under certain circumstances, extra-investment growth factors may be usefully employed. A number of socialist countries are found to have entered a stage when the traditional directive management system tends to be a drag. In such a situation, the first job is to activate sources of growth that were immobilized by the old management system. Then an analysis of the $u$-factor occupies a strategic place in determining the trajectory of further economic development. Special attention will be devoted to this factor in applying Kalecki's model to statistical data (in Chapter VI).

## b) Two basic types of growth models

Research has shown that there is a fundamental difference between a growth model applicable to a capitalist economy and a model applicable to a socialist economy. In a capitalist economy, a decisive influence on growth is exerted primarily by total effective demand, while in a socialist the growth prospects are mainly determined by supply factors. Furthermore, production relations in the widest sense, that is including the given system of planning and management, strongly affect the strategic parameters of the growth model.

True, at first sight there are merely insignificant disparities between, for example, the main features of Kalecki's model and a formula of the Harrod-Domar type. But this agreement is only apparent and the models embody a contradiction in principle. This emerges clearly when the formal relationships among growth factors are subjected to further analysis from the standpoint of the social system in which they operate. Analysis shows that the production relations exert the decisive influence on the strategic parameters of economic growth functions.

In the first place, we find a radical difference in the role of productive investment in the supply-determined socialist economy and the demand-determined capitalist economy. Under socialism, productive investments are the factor destined to expand production capacity and, together with the capital-output ratio, efficiently determine the rate of growth of the national income. In a capitalist economy, however, under the normal conditions of incomplete utilization of the production machine, investments play, according to Keynes, an essentially different macroeconomic role by boosting effective demand.

And it was the Keynesian revolution that propagated the idea in western economics that the prime task of every growth model for capitalism (at least for fully developed capitalism) is to throw light on the complicated conditions under which effective demand might reach a level allowing the factors of production to be fully employed.[10]

The prime task of a growth model for socialism is, on the contrary, much simpler; it should demonstrate the conditions under which production capacity and production may enable society's needs to be met to the maximum. For the economist, the transition from a model applicable to capitalism to one applicable to socialism is a transition from a mysterious realm, in which unsatisfied wants coexist with incompletely utilized production potentials, to a less enigmatic world. Here the sole bounds to maximum satisfaction of society's wants are set by the level of the productive forces and the effectiveness with which they can be utilized.

The new socialist economic conditions enable the problems of growth to be handled from the angle of integrating the goals of the individual and society. It is then possible to choose the optimal distribution of the surplus product in the interests of society's development and to pave the way to reducing the gap between the actual and potential growth rate to a minimum.

By stressing these differences of principle we are far from wishing to maintain that it is an easy matter to steer a socialist economy on a steady course of balanced growth and smooth advance of effectiveness. The de-

---

[10] The American economist P. A. Samuelson has written of this problem of a capitalist economy "We shall see that an industrial system such as our own can do many wonderful things. It can mobilize men, tools, and know-how to respond to any given demand for goods. Over time it can improve upon its own response. But there is one thing it cannot always do. Unless proper policies are pursued, it cannot guarantee that there will be exactly the required amount of investment to ensure full employment ..."

P. A. SAMUELSON, *Economics*, New York, 6th ed. 1964, pp. 207—8

termined search — in the majority of socialist countries — for a model of economic operation embodying intrinsic stimuli to growth confirms that this is an undertaking ranking among the most exacting tasks on the revolutionary road.

In accord with the above fundamental distinction between the two types of growth model, we also find entirely different barriers to growth and different ways of surmounting them. In applying the socialist growth model, we meet with the manpower barrier, the question of setting the permissible rate of net capital formation, the foreign trade barrier (in the sense of import possibilities) etc. In applying the capitalist model, we are concerned with determining an adequate volume of public investment (including public works, armaments programme and an export surplus) and with establishing conditions affording long-term encouragement to the maximum of private investment.

Conjunctural research and the more long-term planning undertaken in a capitalist economy usually deduce the rate of growth of the national income primarily from assumptions about private consumption, private investments, public expenditure and exports. Prognoses as to overall effective demand give the expected growth rate.

Under socialist conditions the situation is reversed. If a certain growth rate is to be achieved, it is primarily necessary to analyse the development of capacities and their coverage by material and manpower resources, and the prospects for import. In this respect the decisive feature for socialist management is economic analysis of supply, i.e. the extent and degree to which productive resources are utilized, while in a capitalist economy the main problems are concentrated in the sphere of total effective demand.

This is far from implying that problems connected with demand, its analysis and prediction, take a back seat in socialist planning. Scientific analysis of the demand structure and its logical changes is the main precondition for rational allocation of the production factors and for timely adaptation of the industrial structure to the needs of the community. This is still more vital in a system of planned management employing a regulated market mechanism. In the economic model, as distinct from the directive system, demand becomes a relatively more independent and important component of economic growth. As a country matures economically and the needs of the population are increasingly satisfied, matters connected with changes in the structure of effective demand acquire growing weight. The need grows for an effective economic mechanism to adapt the structure of production flexibly to that of demand. But the volume of aggregate demand still remains under the overall influence and control of society and it does not play the role of a determinant in economic development that capitalist production relations assign to it.

The differentiation between the growth models applicable to capitalist conditions and those of socialism that has been presented here evidently leads our younger generation of economists to suspect some kind of neo-dogmatism. But they overlook the fact that there is quite a lot in common between Marx's concept of the lack of effective demand under capitalism and Keynes "deflationary gap". And the theory and practice of socialist economics provides sufficient proof that in the new social order — and this is one of its prime virtues — effective demand does not come up against any ceiling, except that of the resources and production capacities available. These remarks are of course no substitute for further research into the points of agreement and disagreement between the role of supply and demand in socialist and capitalist economies, both in the short and long-term, under present conditions.

## c) Growth theory and long-term plan drafting

Growth theory is directly relevant to the fundamental questions, both theoretical and practical, involved in long-term planning. Its guidance is especially valuable in setting the growth rate of the national income. Choice of the growth rate may be considered as the key issue of the perspective plan. In his "Outline of Methods of Compiling the Perspective Plan", M. Kalecki writes: "The average annual growth rate of the national income may be regarded as the most important parameter of long-term planning. Therefore, to choose the correct plan variant means *de facto* to choose the appropriate growth rate for the national income."[11]

The approach to establishing the growth rate is in large measure pre-ordained by the model of socialist economic operation. Every management

---

[11] M. KALECKI, ibid., p. 137.

system has its specific way of handling growth problems and developing the structure of the national income by sectors and branches. A typical feature of every system is its way of unravelling the different problems of growth, that is a kind of growth pattern.

The nature of the directive plan and its place in the centralistic management model in many respects preordains the approach to choosing a growth rate by setting the development rate for individual sectors. This "growth pattern" takes as its starting point the capacity potentials of engineering and building, and the influence of their growth rates is seen in the expected volume of investment. From this follow claims on the growth rates of metallurgy, fuel extraction, electric power and demands on foreign trade. The limits are thereby set for production by other manufacturing industries and for non-productive consumption.

This "growth pattern", which is to a greater or lesser degree inherent in the administrative-directive management model, derives the resultant growth rate of the national income primarily from the envisaged rate of development in individual sectors, thus shaping the industrial structure of the national income. However, the objective correlations of the socialist reproduction process are apprehended by this means in incorrect relationships and the planning procedure evolves the resultant growth rate of the national income in the opposite direction to that required by the objective course of balanced economic growth. The precondition for a balanced, economically justifiable growth rate is to select a base variant of growth for the national income that through the final structure of consumption will definitely determine the industrial structure of the national product.

The opposite approach — deriving the growth rate of the national income from the assumed industrial structure of the national income — is, on the other hand, linked with voluntarism.

However paradoxical it may seem, the voluntarism follows from the fact that a central planning authority should not lay down the industrial structure at all. As Kalecki has shown,[12] in fact a central planning authority has no freedom of choice, or almost no freedom, with regard to the industrial structure of the national income, or more precisely of the national product. That is to say, the target structure of the national product is

12 M. KALECKI, ibid., p. 150.

already bound to follow from the target level of the national income. From the planned overall growth in national income over the plan period we obtain the target structure of consumption by means of coefficients of income elasticity of demand. Then, from the target structure of consumption we get, through technical coefficients and the input-output table, the target structure of production.

So we see that the target industrial structure of the national income necessarily derives from the planned growth rate and consumption structure and not from any subjective decision-making. With regard to the industrial structure of the national product, the central planning authority, therefore, has no obligation to choose the structure or to optimalize it. Its sole duty is to have scientific knowledge of the industrial structure deriving from the total target level of the national income and to realize it in the plan, i.e. incorporate it correctly in the plan.

We believe that there are indisputable optimalization criteria for choosing among various variants within one sector. There is usually a considerable degree of variability within a sector or branch with regard to choosing the most suitable techniques and technological methods. Here a wide field is offered for plan optimalization, because one and the same product can usually be made with various combinations of capital and labour intensity.

On the other hand, in a closed economy there are no optimalization criteria, and variants are entirely lacking with regard to distribution of investment means to individual sectors of the economy.

There are two exceptions to this principle. Firstly, the central planning authority possesses some freedom of decision with regard to public consumption, investment in the infrastructure and other so-called nonproductive investments. Within limits, proportions can be chosen freely here, or more exactly, they can be chosen from the angle of various social priorities.

The second exception is that the above principle is only valid in a closed model. In the case of an open model, i.e. when external economic relationships are taken into account, the central planning authority has freedom of decision in further areas. It can decide in the light of calculations covering the effectiveness of the whole national economy whether anti-import or pro-export investments will be most suitable. Otherwise calculations of investment effectiveness are applicable only to the choice among variants within a given sector.

"In general we may state that the industrial structure of the national income is determined:

a)  by the rate of its growth,
b)  by the final structure of consumption and its relation to nonproductive investments,
c)  by assessing the effectiveness of alternative production methods and by foreign trade policy."[13]

Nonetheless, our account has been rather schematic. Things are not in reality so simple. While the central planning authority lacks freedom of decision in the given areas (with the exceptions mentioned), it has quite a difficult and responsible job in choosing, for example, the Engel coefficients for the long-term; more precisely, in making statistical estimates of coefficients valid for a long period and in choosing technological coefficients for input-output tables. The question also arises whether empirically determined technological coefficients will be valid over the whole plan period and whether, in any event, it is possible to assume their linearity.

Traditional planning practice, to which the principle that the target structure of the national income is preordained is unknown, leads to serious consequences. Such planning procedures throw the door wide open to infringing the principles of rational operation, with shortages developing in some sectors and surpluses in others as a result. The shortfall in some sectors is not always met by adjusting the rates of growth in allied sectors; instead, the surpluses from the latter are kept in reserve, often with no consideration as to whether such commodities are really needed. Kalecki has aptly remarked about such planning methods: "The approach is wrong, because it leads to the need for some products being overestimated already in the plan, or to labelling surpluses of such products as reserves. Naturally, reserves in the plan are very useful, but they should be formed at the danger points... and not by chance, just to maintain a high indicator as a symbol of progress. In reality, however, such tolerating of 'surplus' indicators leads to squandering either by inflating need in the plan, or by allowing for un-

[13]  M. KALECKI, ibid., p. 150.

necessary reserves that 'wet the appetite' and may be the cause of increased needs during plan fulfilment."[14]

A rate of growth chosen in the traditional manner in the light of the anticipated structure of the national income usually enables relatively high increments in production to be planned, but it also encourages reproduction of bottle-necks, accompanied by surpluses of other products. When demand is unsatisfied, the market in the end absorbs such surpluses. But as the industrial level rises and the market becomes more saturated, this unilateral approach to choice of a growth rate for the national income, combined with the effects of the directive management model, is manifested in increasing waste of social labour.

[14] M. KALECKI, ibid., p. 151.

Chapter III

# Short-term Variations in the Growth Rate of a Socialist Economy

In this chapter an exposition of quasi-cyclical movements in the rate of economic growth and in some further macro-economic data is presented, relating to Czechoslovakia and some other socialist countries of similar economic structure. An attempt is made to identify the mechanism calling forth such fluctuations, primarily in the investment cycle, the inventory cycle and the correlated cycle in the foreign trade balance.

Analysis of the dynamics of industrial production and investment activity in Czechoslovakia, Poland, the GDR and Hungary supplies an interesting picture (*Diagram No. 1*). The rate of growth of industrial production shows relatively regular fluctuations,[1] with maximum increments of output in the years 1951 – 1952 and 1959 – 1960, and minimum increments in the years 1953 – 1955 and 1961 – 1963. In 1963 there actually was a fall in industrial production in Czechoslovakia. However, in 1964 a new period of accelerated growth began. These fluctuations are still more pronounced if the analysis is confined to producer goods. In the period investigated, variability of investment activity, and synchronization of its oscillations are

---

[1]  The problem of variations in the rate of growth has already been dealt with by Prof. B. MINC, *Ekonomista* (1962), no. 3; Prof. JULIO H. G. OLIVERA, *Kyklos* (1960), no. 2; Prof. M. ČOBELJIĆ and Prof. RADMILA STOJANOVIĆ, *Ekonomist* (1961), no. 4; Prof. G. J. STALLER, *American Economic Review* (1964), no. 3; R. CHELIŃSKI, *Ekonomista* (1964), pp. 1045 – 1056. Following our first analysis of this problem in September 1964, some more work was published: J. PAJESTKA, *Analysis of Some Aspects of Polish Economic Development Policy* (An Investigation into the Phasing of Economic Growth), Warsaw, Research Institute of State Planning Commission; Prof. BRANKO HORVAT: "Economic Cycle in Yugoslavia", *Ekonomist* (1966), no. 1—4; AGNIESZKA KLISZKO: "An Attempt of Verification of the Hypothesis of an Investment Cycle in Poland", *Gospodarka planowa* (1967), no. 7. N. ČOBELJIĆ - R. STOJANOVIĆ, *The Theory of the Investment Cycle in a Socialist Economy*, Belgrade 1966.

even more striking. The mechanism of fluctuations in the growth rate may be described as follows.

**No. 1. Rate of growth of investments in Czechoslovakia, Poland and Hungary 1950 to 1966**

(Annual increments of decrements, in %; constant prices except for Hungary).

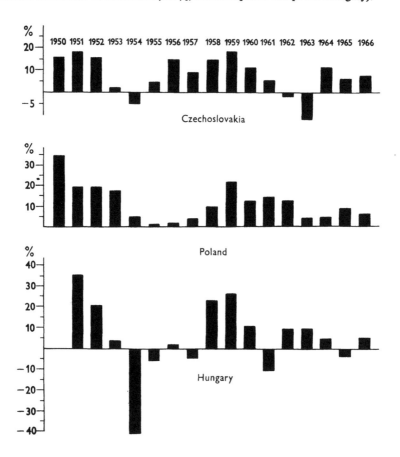

## a) The mechanism of fluctuations

As shown by Professor Michal Kalecki[2], in a relatively small, industrially developed socialist country there is a tendency for the raw-material base to lag behind the growth of manufacturing industries whenever the rate of growth exceeds a certain optimum level. Such development is due to a tendency for underfulfilment of production (and investment) plans in the extracting and basic materials industries and for overfulfilment of such plans in the higher-stage manufacturing industries, resulting in the formation of what has come to be known as the raw-material barrier. This in turn will bring about additional imbalances in the foreign trade balance. That barrier, likewise, is bound to slow down economic growth, particularly in a relatively small country with limited domestic raw-material resources.

In the given context, agriculture is playing a similar role as the basic industries mentioned above, in view of the economic and social factors making for slow growth in this industry. Thus, the relatively slow development of agriculture will cause additional strain and disproportions whenever the overall growth rate exceeds the rate of balanced growth.

The disproportions and acute economic difficulties, ensuing from an above-optimum rate of growth, can only be overcome by slowing down the pace of economic development. This breathing period will continue until new investment projects, initiated in the preceding period, predominantly in the 'basic' industries, will successively mature and go into operation. As a result of both the slow-down in growth, in industrial output and in investment activity, and the contribution of new output facilities, the supply situation will gradually improve. Thus, conditions will be set up which — through a certain voluntarism inherent in the traditional system of planning and management — will permit such a quasi-cycle to restart again.

As to the interrelation between objective and subjective factors in the genesis of quasi-cyclical movement in the rate of growth, the following conclusion may be drawn from the analysis given above. The phase of decelera-

---

[2] *Zarys teorii wzrostu gospodarki socjalisticznej*, Warsaw 1963, pp. 51—53; Prof. K. LASKI, *Zarys teorii reprodukcji socjalistycznej*, Warsaw, 1963, pp. 426—505; *Problems in Economic Dynamics Planning — in Honour of Michal Kalecki*, Warsaw 1964, pp. 59—78.

tion is objectively unavoidable. Once disproportions have been allowed to develop rather far in a planning system, reacting only indirectly and with some time-lag to market signals, they cannot be overcome otherwise than by reducing the rate of growth. Things are more complicated as far as acceleration is concerned. Certain subjectivist tendencies towards maximizing the rate of growth assert themselves continuously. However, it is only under conditions such as prevailed about 1950 or 1959 (conditions like those in the latter year may reoccur cyclically, as happened in 1966–1967), that voluntarism in planning has an exceptionally wide field of action. The process of acceleration, though ensuing from subjective and subjectivist decision-making, nevertheless has its specific objective foundation.

## b)  Historical retrospect

Historically, the fluctuations in the growth rate in the four countries under review developed as follows. The success of economic planning in the period of postwar reconstruction and the gradual release of large output and labour-productivity reserves in those years, in conjunction with the deterioration of the international situation, resulted in 1950–1951 in the revision of current plans (or plan projects) with a view to a considerable rise in the rate of economic growth far beyond the optimum level. The economic difficulties and disproportions following from such development could only be overcome by a heavy cut in the rate of growth and in the volume of investment (1953 to 1954). The radical economic measures of that period were not so much due to political changes; they were, in fact, the unavoidable outcome of the preceding economic development. Making possible the solution of the disproportions inherited from the preceding period, they simultaneously set up the indispensable preconditions for the implementation of the "New Deal" after Stalins' death.

After a gradual recovery beginning from 1954, a new period of very rapid development started about 1958. At that time many investment projects, initiated in the early fifties, particularly in the basic industries, were completed and put into full operation, playing a decisive part in overcoming or substantially alleviating the economic disproportions that had brought about the fall in the rate of growth in 1953 and 1954. All available data show that 1958, as the years 1950–51, was one of the most successful years in the history of economic planning.

However, these objective conditions, in conjunction with certain subjectivist tendencies inherent in the traditional model of economic planning and management, gave rise to a new wave of industrialization and a new investment drive, culminating about 1959–1960. For reasons mentioned above, such development necessarily caused – or aggravated – disproportions, such as had once before made their appearance in 1953–54, and induced a similar, though far steeper decline in the rate of growth of industrial production in the period 1961–63. While in Czechoslovakia there was still a fall in output in the latter year, a notable consolidation has since taken place.

## c)   The investment cycle and the effects of overinvestment

The loss of proportionality, ensuing from a rate of growth in excess of the optimum level, will be intensified in its results by the well-known effect of overinvestment, induced or necessitated by the selected rate of growth. Overinvestment is not an independent cause of the decline in the rate of growth, but one of the factors accompanying excessive growth. However, in the development of the Czechoslovak economy, for instance, tension, due to an excessive rate of output growth, is intensified by the effects of overinvestment. When a new investment wave is started, additional strain is caused in an economy in which there already operate disequilibrating forces, resulting from an excessive rate of output growth. Thus, general deceleration becomes unavoidable to restore equilibrium.

With a time-lag of about eight or nine years, corresponding to the length of the construction and gestation period under given conditions, the same investment wave will bring about an opposite affect. With the peak reached in the increments of the flow of new fixed assets coming into operation as a result of investments projects, started previously, particularly in the extractive and basic industries, the supply situation will improve, and the system will tend towards equilibrium. It is thus the investment cycle which gives the operation of the raw-material barrier its specific oscillating character. (See *Diagram No. 2.*)

### No. 2. Mechanism of Wave-Like Movements in Growth Rate

(The echo-effect of investment waves in new-output-capacities flow in growth rate of producers goods industries, and in inventory formation)

1. *Changes in investment activity* (year-to-year changes, percentages)

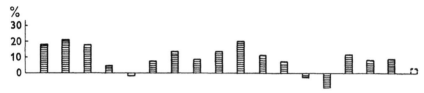

2. *Increments in flow of new fixed assets, going into operation in industry* (billion Kčs)

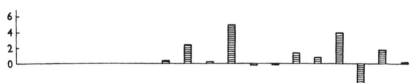

3. *Growth rate of output of producers goods industries* (percentages)

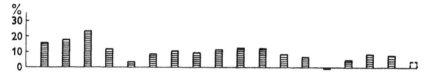

4. *Changes in inventories* (year-to-year changes, billion Kčs)

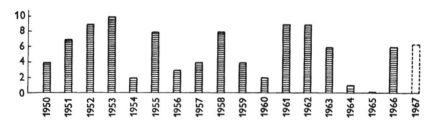

Fluctuations in investment activity (first line) give rise to an echo-effect in two significant peaks in the increments of the flow of new industrial capacities, with a time-lag of about eight or nine years (second line). There is fairly satisfactory synchronization of the above wave-like movements with the rate of growth of the output of producers goods industries (third line). A further echo-effect of the investment cycle, shows up in significant changes in inventory formation (fourth line).

**Sources:**
Economic Growth in Czechoslovakia, pp. 36, 37, 44, 68.
**Note:** Data for 1967 are estimated.

## d) Inventory cycle

Although both the immediate disequilibrating effect and the equilibrating echo-effect of investment waves have a primary function in generating fluctuations, another, though secondary, factor seems to be of still greater importance. We are referring to variations in inventory formation which, induced by quasicyclical changes in the relation between supply and effective demand, at the same time, intensify them to a very large extent. (See again *Diagram No. 2.*) In those years when the increase in the flow of investment in new industrial capacity is at a maximum, the supply position is improving. Enterprises will adjust themselves to such a change by lowering their inventory-turnover ratios, thus alleviating further the supply position in the economy as a whole. As a result, there will arise a strong tendency toward reduction of inventories. The successive improvements in the supply position are thus characterized by a positive feedback effect, and the process of relative or absolute disaccumulation of stocks will gain momentum.

When, however, under conditions of relative economic equilibrium, the rate of growth of industrial output expands again, new tension and strain develop with a resultant deterioration in the supply position. Enterprises adjust themselves to such changes by raising their inventory-turnover ratios, thus worsening still more the supply position in the economy as a whole. As a result, the growth rate will decline.

Such unfavourable developments will come to an end only when the combined effect of the falling rate of growth and a new peak in the increments of the flow of new fixed capital again alleviates tension and strain, easing the supply position.

There is an interesting time-lag problem. Inventory investment reaches a maximum at a point when the growth rate of output has passed its peak. This fact, however, seems to be in agreement with the thesis that it is inventory investment which, with a kind of multiplier effect, reinforces the deceleration in the growth of output which would follow from the fading of the echo-effect (of changes in investment activity) in the flow of new fixed assets in industry.

The time-lag of inventory investment behind the industrial growth rate is not only apparent in the phase of deceleration of industrial growth. Though lagged correlation is not so close in this case, the lag appears in the phase of accelerated industrial growth as well. Industrial growth is already accelerating when inventory formation is near a minimum. This fact seems to be in line with the above interpretation that the causal nexus works primarily from inventory investment toward the rate of output growth, and not the other way round.

However, the behaviour of enterprises described above and sometimes referred to as a kind of "socialist speculation" is not as irrational as might appear at first sight from the macroeconomic point of view.

An enterprise will carefully balance the costs and risks of minimizing inventories against the expenses incurred by holding excessive inventories. The smoother the supply (and transport) situation, the lower will it be possible to hold the inventory-turnover ratio, optimizing this relation on the basis of economic calculations.

The behaviour of enterprises — particularly under conditions of the new system of economic planning and management — is influenced not so much by given conditions in the sphere of supply of raw materials and goods in process as by expectations relating to future developments. Increasing uncertainty as to further developments in the supply position may in itself bring about unfavourable developments. Expectations, being subjective factors, may in themselves become objective factors determining the development of real economic processes.

### e) Combined effect of investment and inventory cycles

In the following, an attempt is made quantitatively to examine the joint impact of synchronized investment and inventory cycles, both on economic equilibrium and the resulting rate of growth. In addition, inventory changes are investigated together with changes in the volume of capital-under-construction which are likewise synchronized with the investment cycle. Within the cycle, the average age of capital-under-construction varies significantly: It is considerably reduced when a large number of new projects is started with the foundation of a new investment wave, at the peak of the cycle, and notably raised when in the through phase new investment is curtailed and completed projects go into operation.

The decelerating effect of excessive accumulation of inventories and capital-under-construction — and the accelerating effect of disaccumulation — can be shown by an incremental analysis, using year-to-year changes in accumulation data. In 1961, for instance, of the increment in national income (of about fifteen billion crowns), approximately two-thirds was used to increase accumulation and about one-third to increase consumption. The expansion of accumulation into inventories and capital-under-construction was, however, larger than the rise in consumption or in fixed capital accumulation, net of capital-under-construction (that is in other words the increment in the flow of new fixed assets going into operation).

In this respect, there is an import analogy between economic developments in 1966 and in 1961. In 1966, as in 1961, the expansion of accumulation into inventories and capital-under-construction was larger than the increase in consumption or the increase in fixed capital formation, net of capital-under-construction.

But in 1964, developments constrasted sharply with those in 1961 or in 1966. In 1964, the increase in national income was far smaller than — but the increase in consumption was as large as — for instance, the corresponding figure in 1966. This was due to the fact that in 1964 there was a large decrease in accumulation into inventories and capital-under-construction. In 1964, the combination of a fairly high rate of increase in consumption with a relatively low rate of growth of national income was not achieved — as many economists believed — at the cost of accumulation of fixed capital, net of capital-under-construction. On the contrary, fixed capital brought into operation rose by more than 5 billion crowns. Such a development, which at first sight seems somewhat inconsistent, was made possible by a disaccumulation of excessively high inventories and of capital-under-construction. As a result "disposable" national income (that is national income reduced by a rise in the volume of inventories and capital-under-construction, or increased for a decline) was considerably higher than national income according to the current definition. On the other hand, in 1961 and 1966, disposable national income was considerably lower than national income as currently defined, for the reason that the rate of increase of inventories and capital-under-construction was high. (See *Diagrams No. 3 and 4.*)

If the process of reproduction is compared with a pipeline, into which there enter the factors of production and from which there flow final prod-

**No. 3. Relationship Between "Statistical" and "Disposable" National Income**

(Balance between increments in "statistical"*) and in "disposable" national**) income)

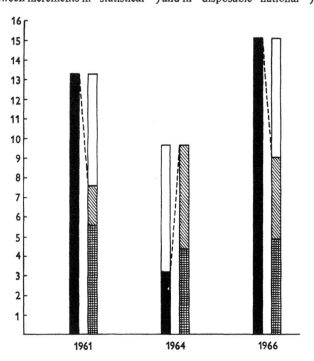

Increments in:

■ "Statistical" national income

☐ Accumulation in inventories and capital under construction

▦ Consumption

▨ Flow of new fixed assets, going into operation in industry

– – – Broken line is to draw attention to differences between "statistical" and "disposable" national income increments

**Source:** Economic Growth in Czechoslovakia, Prague, 1966, p. 68.

*) Statistical national income: national income as currently defined in Czechoslovakia.

**) Disposable national income: national income reduced for the increase (or increased for the decline) in volume of inventories and capital under construction

No. 4.  **Quasi-cyclical Changes in Relationship Between "Statistical" and "Disposable" National Income: The Pipe-line Effect**

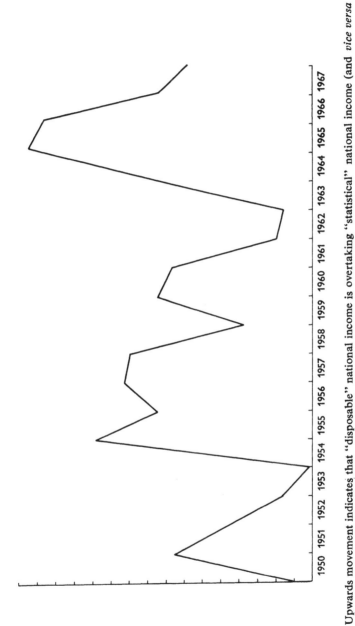

Upwards movement indicates that "disposable" national income is overtaking "statistical" national income (and *vice versa* for downward movement). In other words, upward movement indicates release from and downward movement damming-up in pipe-line.

**Note:** Interval on vertical scale represents 1 billion crowns.

ucts, either for consumption or for raising the volume of productive and "nonproductive" capacity in operation, then it may be said that in 1967 (as in 1961) there was a large increase − relative to factor input − in the volume of the factors of production inside the pipeline. For this reason, the output of final products for consumption or fixed capital formation was relatively low as compared with the input of factors of production.

On the other hand, in 1964 an opposite process was in operation. Inventories and capital-under-construction declined. Therefore, the output of final products was considerably larger than might have been expected from the input of factors of production.

Thus, the accumulation of inventories and of capital under construction represents one of the main factors which make for alternating intensification and alleviation of economic tension, for intensification or alleviation of economic imbalance, and for the resultant fluctuations in the rate of economic growth.

## f) The interrelation between the raw-material and foreign-trade barriers

Our analysis has been confined so far to a closed model, abstracting from the effects of foreign trade. In a further approximation to reality, the interrelation between the raw-material and foreign-trade barriers has to be taken into account. In fact, both barriers form a system of interconnected vessels with a specific behaviour within the quasicycle. From our *Diagram No. 5*, a fairly close correlation is apparent between changes in the rate of growth of imports of raw materials and semi-manufactures, and changes in the rate of growth of producer goods industries. The variation in the import series is, however, far larger than that in the output series. From the difference between these magnitudes, the elasticity of the demand for imports of raw-materials and semi-manufactures may be estimated at 2·0, approximately.

A rise in exports, sufficient in size to cover rapidly rising import requirements, is rather difficult to achieve at short notice. This applies particularly to exports to Western countries, where the major part of additional import requirements has to be obtained since the exchange of goods between socialist countries is planned, and carried out, on a long-term basis. These are the main reasons why in a period of acceleration "scissors" are opening between import requirements and export possibilities. The resulting need for import restrictions in the peak phase of the quasicycle thus reinforces the operation of the raw-material barrier, as mentioned above, and supplies additional motives for inventory hoarding.

**No. 5. Foreign Trade Barrier in Quasi-cyclical Movement**

1. Growth rate of output of producers goods industries (percentages).

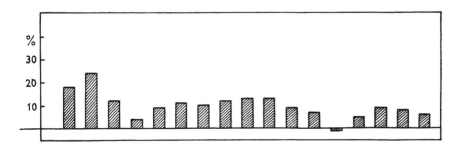

2. Growth rate of import of raw materials and semi-manufactured goods (percentages).

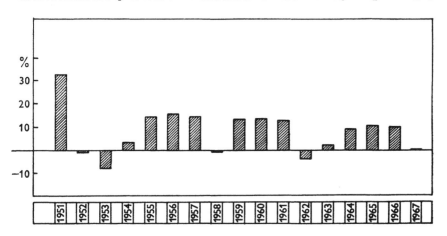

Note: Data for 1967 are estimated.

An analogous argument applies to the transition into the trough phase of the quasicycle. With a declining rate of growth for industrial output, import requirements for raw-materials and semi-manufactures will decelerate to a far greater extent. In other words, the pressure on the foreign trade balance will tend to lessen, with the result that the supply position will improve not only for the reasons given in previous sections, but also in respect of foreign supplies.[3] Such development will set up the conditions for (relative or absolute) inventory disinvestment on the part of the enterprises, again with a positive feedback effect making the process self-perpetuating in the subsequent period of acceleration.

On closer examination, our diagram shows a time-lag, approximately of one year, between two time-series. Changes in the rate of growth for raw-materials and semi-manufactures lead before the changes in the growth rate of output. This was only to be expected in view of the need of securing deliveries of input material in advance of actual requirements, and because of the given length of the production period.

## g) Summary

As a result of our analysis so far, the presentation of the mechanism of wave-like movements in the growth rate (*Diagram No. 2*) may be summarized as follows:

The top section of the diagram presents data on year-to-year changes in investment activity, covering two full cycles. In the second section, the echo-effect of these fluctuations is shown in two significant peaks in the increments of the flow of new investment in industrial capacity. With a time-lag of about eight or nine years, corresponding to the length of the construction and gestation period under given conditions, the two peaks in investment activity at about 1951 – 52 and 1959 – 60 are reflected in similar peaks in the increments of the flow of new fixed assets coming into operation in industry in the 1959 – 60 and 1964 – 67 periods.

---

[3] Cf. Prof. K. LASKI, "The Influence of Foreign Trade on the Rate of Economic Growth" in *International Trade and Development Theory and Policy*, Warsaw 1966, pp. 88 – 111.

The third section in the diagram indicates a fairly satisfactory synchronization of this wave-like movement, both in investment activity and the flow of new fixed capital, with the rate of growth of the output of producer goods industries.

Finally, the last section presents a further echo-effect of the investment cycle, appearing in significant inventory changes that are due to expectations relating to further developments in the supply position. When the increase in the flow of new industrial capacity is at a maximum, enterprises will adjust themselves to such an improvement in the supply position by lowering their inventory-turnover ratios, thus alleviating further the supply position in the economy as a whole. In this way a positive feedback effect will come into operation, and the process of relative or absolute disaccumulation of stocks will gain momentum, with a resulting tendency towards economic equilibrium and a rise in the rate of growth.

The inventory cycle is reinforced by − and interacts with − a parallel cycle in the foreign trade balance, as far as import requirements (for raw-materials and semi-manufactures) are concerned. The latter accelerate more rapidly than the output growth rate in the up-swing, and decelerate more rapidly in the down-swing. Thus, additional disequilibrating forces are brought into operation in one phase and additional equilibrating forces in the other. As a result, the system will reach a turning point in the quasi-cyclical movement: the upper one in the former case, and the lower one in the latter, due to the joint operation of the inventory cycle and the cycle in the foreign trade balance.

## h) Economic fluctuations under socialism and under capitalism

The exposition of quasi-cyclical movement in the growth rate of Czechoslovakia (and some other socialist countries) may be taken to corroborate the theory of convergence of the two social systems. It is true that fluctuations in the growth rate may be observed in some socialist, as well as in capitalist countries; however, the wave-like movement in the rate of growth, analysed above, obviously differs in principle from cyclical development under capitalism. While a fall in output is quite exceptional under socialism, quarterly, if not annual, data show that a decline occurs more or less regularly in developed capitalist countries, particularly in the United States, Canada, Scandinavia, etc.

In the postwar period, capitalist countries succeeded in alleviating the amplitude of cyclical fluctuations carrying out an active and complex economic policy, which is based upon what has become to be known as the new economics.[4] It is true, of course, that local wars, and particularly war preparations were important factors in raising effective demand — directly in some countries and indirectly, via foreign trade in others. Thus, a relatively stable rate of growth could be achieved over a fairly long period. Nevertheless, few economists in the West hold that, under capitalism, the trade cycle is already obsolete. One need not be a dogmatist to maintain that the economic cycle follows from the economic and social structure of the capitalist system and, in practice, can only be mitigated by state intervention.[5]

On the other hand, fluctuations in the rate of growth in our conditions ensue from insufficient knowledge of the economic laws of socialism and from shortcomings in their application.

Selection of optimum rates of growth, coupled with a thorough overhaul of the system of economic planning and management, and elimination of a relapse into overinvestment, would contribute to the prevention of economic overstrain and disproportions that otherwise might arise again in the future. Thus, it might be possible to secure more regular and, in the long run, more rapid economic growth. Since fluctuations appear to be due to gnoseological reasons in one case and to structural factors in the other, the term quasi-cycle has been applied to fluctuations in a socialist economy.

The basic causes of both deceleration and acceleration are linked to the development of the relation between supply and effective demand, under capitalism as well as under socialism. While, however, in a capitalist economy deceleration is due, as a rule, to deficiency of effective demand, the opposite applies to a socialist economy. There, deceleration is due to economic strain and tension which ensue from the lagging of supply under

---

[4]  PAUL A. SAMUELSON, *Economics*, New York, 1962, 6th ed., pp. 265, 786, 7, 150, 264, 337—38.

[5]  Cf. PAUL A. SAMUELSON, "Problems of the American Economy — Hard and Easy" in *New Horizons of Economic Progress*, Detroit 1964, pp. 33—36.

the intensified operation of the raw material, foreign trade, and production-capacity barriers.

It is for this reason that the way out of the trough in the growth rate (i.e., the transition into acceleration) differs, in principle, in capitalism and socialism. Under the classical model of Marx, acceleration will start when the moral and physical *Verschleiss* of fixed productive capital gradually balances the relation between supply and demand; under modern conditions, acceleration will be brought about by coordinated application of the new instruments of economic policy, including local wars and more intensive war preparations. Under socialism, the transition into acceleration is rendered possible, first of all, by maturing production capacities, the construction of which was started in the period centering about the peak of the preceding investment cycle. Thus, supply is increased while simultaneously the fairly low rate of growth (and low investment activity) reduces demand relative to supply, particularly in the basic branches of industry.

An analogous argument applies to the transition into deceleration. Under capitalism, maturing investment projects accentuate the excess of supply relative to effective demand, thus strengthening the basic contradiction of capitalism. Under socialism, the excess of effective demand is accentuated at the peak of the quasi-cycle by maximal investment activity, connected with an increase in the volume of capital under construction. Thus, in both social systems there are analogous processes, proceeding, however, in opposite directions.

The inventory cycle, and the cycle in the foreign trade balance, analysed above, apparently increase the amplitude of fluctuations in both social systems. In this field, too, cyclical development again operates, as a rule, in opposite directions. Under capitalism, inventories are reduced in the initial phase of a decline (or deceleration) in output, further increasing supply, compared with current output.[6] In a socialist economy, inventories rise steeply at this phase, as a result of the speculative tendencies mentioned above, which accentuate the excess of effective demand.

This argument, however, needs some qualification. There are quite frequently cases in which capitalist countries with a limited natural resources endowment and, consequently, a high import dependence, come up against

---

[6] SAMUELSON, *op. cit.*, p. 257.

the foreign trade barrier, bringing to an end the up-swing in the growth rate. In this connection it may be interesting to note that economic fluctuations in the countries investigated seem to be to some extent synchronized with cyclical movement, say in Great Britain or the Netherlands, where peak-periods show up around 1950, 1960, and 1964, while there was, however, an additional peak in 1954. Such a rather mysterious case of convergence, in what might seem to amount to international transmission of economic fluctuations between the two social systems, would represent an interesting field for further investigation.

Chapter IV

# Long-term Variations in the Growth Rate

"... to predict means simply to have a good view of the present and the past as movement. To have a good view means to distinguish exactly the basic and constant elements of the process."

ANTONIO GRAMSCI

This chapter is devoted to an examination of the causes underlying long-term deceleration of growth, seen in relation to the model of management concerned. Examination of the influence exerted by the directive administrative system of management may seem rather an academic occupation now that a new economic system is in course of introduction. But the reform should not be regarded as purely an administrative undertaking confined to issuing legal regulations which the executive can then implement, perhaps with the support of some explanation and propaganda. As Prof. O. Lange was probably the first to underline, a profound social transformation is involved, actually taking place within the sphere of socialist production relations, where the general public interest is bound to clash with group interests.

The group interests stem from rights and authority acquired close on two decades ago. In the meantime, the habits of what is now a traditional mode of thought have been built up, and today they hinder the change-over to new methods of management. As a rule, the people concerned are not fully aware of such conflicting interests; the obstacle lies more in the realm of cognition, preventing those who have been working for a long time in planning and management from really appreciating the inevitability of the changes now underway. This is all the more true when we realize that for central and sectoral planners the successes of the first Soviet Five-Year Plans are indissolubly linked with the system of planned management. Similarly, they are strongly influenced by the fact that in Czechoslovakia and the other people's democracies, too, socialist industrialization proceeded under the aegis of the traditional system of planned management, and the successes of this phase are again linked with the system.

What is more, it was still no easy matter in the second half of the fifties to make any radical criticism of the traditional methods of planning and management. Even Western economists had not managed to gain a clear picture of how long they could operate and how far they were tied to specific economic and political situations. Moreover, at that time economists in the West were little concerned with models as we know them today, and were more interested in enquiring how long it would take for the world socialist system (still governed by the traditional model of planned management) to catch up with the capitalist world.

All this has to be taken into account in order to understand why the present changes have come comparatively late. This insight can also help to win support for rapid implementation of the new system. In this connection we shall deal here with the influence of the old methods on the process of economic growth over the past fifteen years.

The valuable discussion on the system that took place in 1963−64 tended to be conducted at two levels, either more or less academic and theoretical, or with a healthy, but inadequate practicism, chiefly directed at criticizing the many absurdities inevitably bred by the old system.

If this system was indeed a product of its day, shaped by the economic and political conditions prevailing at its birth, we arrive at the paradoxical conclusion that the fruits of the "cult" in this sphere were often countered by instruments typical for the economic thinking of the past. All who have been trying to overcome the out-dated forms of planned management have long been operating with a legacy of mere deduction, which can readily be taken for speculation, or mere induction, which may give the impression of casuistry.

But the now generally accepted conclusion of several generations of economists, and a notable feature of the methods employed by the founders of Marxism-Leninism, is an intimate linking of deduction and induction by means of quantitative analysis, using statistical methods. One of the unfortunate consequences of the "cult" was to cut short the development of Marxist economics in the Soviet Union in this field. Economists who want to overcome the consequences of the recent past are therefore faced with the job of rehabilitating quantitative analysis; in the last few years, for example, attempts have been made in Czechoslovakia by people working in the fields of inter-sectoral relationships and linear programming, to demand functions, theories of economic growth etc.

The keynote of this chapter is as follows: The traditional system was at bottom fitted to conditions of "exténsive" development and accelerated industrialization under which it arose in the Soviet Union. To a degree, similar conditions existed in Czechoslovakia, Poland, Hungary and the German Democratic Republic at the time when planned economy was introduced, to be precise, in 1950 – 52, when – sometimes in an overthorough and rigid manner – the centralized administrative system was introduced according to the Soviet model. As the potentialities of further "extensive" development were gradually exhausted and the change-over to the "intensive" course came to be essential, the inaptness of the given model of socialist economic operation to the underlying economic conditions grew at an equal rate. The attempt here made to analyse the economic consequences of this discrepancy between development of the productive forces and management system[1] cannot pretend – in common with the analysis in the foregoing chapter – to do more than pose the problem and provide some impulse to a somewhat broader discussion of what is a foremost issue for the Czechoslovak economy – and not for the Czechoslovak alone.

## a) Decline of dynamic

The growth dynamic of industrial production in Czechoslovakia, Poland, Hungary and the German Democratic Republic reveals, alongside the more or less periodic fluctuations already examined, a mildly decelerating trend. And in the long-view, the rate of growth is the decisive criterion for assessing the plan and its implementation (See *Diagram 6.*)

As shown in Table 3, the second peak of the growth rate (around 1959) was lower than the maximum of 1951 or 1952, the 1962 – 3 growth rates were lower (with the exception of Hungary) than the minimum for 1954 – 6. Similarly, the maximum to date in the third peak phase of wave movement is again lower than around 1959.

---

[1]  See *Problémy nové soustavy plánování a financování čs. průmyslu* (Problems of the New System of Planning and Financing Czechoslovak Industry), Prague 1957, pp. 11 – 15.

**Table 3.** *Extreme values in the wave movement of the growth rate of industrial output (annual increments — %)*

| | 1950 (maximum) | 1956 (minimum) | 1960 (maximum) | 1963 (minimum) | 1965 (maximum) to date |
|---|---|---|---|---|---|
| Czechoslovakia | 16·7* | 4·0** | 11·9 | —0·6 | 7·9 |
| GDR | 28·5 | 6·0 | 12·0*** | 4·3 | 6·6+ |
| Poland | 28·3 | 8·8 | 10·7 | 5·5 | 9·3+ |
| Hungary | 28·8 | —9·2 | 12·8 | 7·1 | 8·8+ |

\* 1952, ** 1954, *** 1959, + 1964, growth rate in 1965 lower.

**No. 6. Long-term decline of industrial growth rate**
(sliding averages with seven-year base).

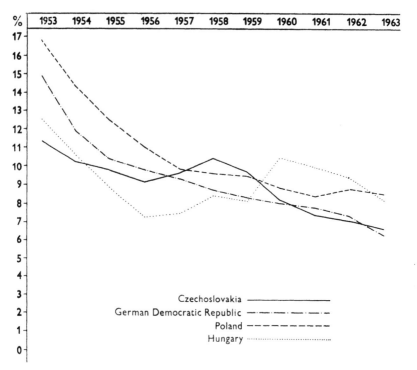

Czechoslovakia ——————
German Democratic Republic —·—·—·—·—·
Poland ——————
Hungary ·················

A similar phenomenon was to be observed in Soviet industrial development from the first to third Five-Year Plans, which actuated Stalin's treatment of this question at the Eighteenth Congress of the Soviet Communist Party in 1939. Although Soviet industry still maintains a fairly high growth rate, deceleration can be observed again in the recent phase following the completion of postwar reconstruction, but the trend is less pronounced than in the above countries.[2]

## Retarding factors — secondary and primary

We frequently hear in discussions that deceleration of growth is induced by factors such as progressive exhaustion of reserves, the distorting influence of the gross output indicator and the existence of highly-developed productive forces ("stagnation theory").

As far as reserves are concerned, the long-term decline in the four socialist countries under consideration can be partly accounted for by the well-known fact that the considerable reserves in capacities, manpower and productivity existing in the early fifties generated an exceptionally high rate.

Some part is also played in the given circumstances by the fact that the indicator used to measure the rate of growth, i.e. gross output, somewhat distorts the actual development. The resultant error is in fact larger for the first years of development than for the more recent, so that the statistically determined drop is to some extent purely optical as a result of increasing precision of the indicator.

Attempts are sometimes made to apply the stagnation theory, or more accurately, the theory of inevitability of growth deceleration, which originated in the capitalist context, to the divergent conditions of socialist economic growth. Attention is called to the fact that as they approach the "degree of maturity" of the advanced capitalist countries, the socialist countries will be forced to slow down their growth rates and statistics are advanced to confirm the correctness of these views.

---

[2]  Annual increments, 1950—1966 (plan): percentages 23, 16, 12, 12, 13, 12, 11, 10, 10, 11, 10, 9, 10, 9, 7, 9, (7).

However, it seems that not one of the three factors mentioned above as explanations of the deceleration really represent the true causes.

While there is no doubt that the reserves set free by the revolutionary change in the relations of production generated the higher growth rates of the early fifties, this factor should not be overestimated in an analysis of the causes of long-term deceleration. Insofar as the resources made available by the change-over to a more progressive social order were fairly easily mobilized, they were already substantially exhausted by about 1953 in the key sectors. Mobilization of the other reserves from this source is then a long-term process, as can be demonstrated, for example, by figures on improving the extensive utilization of capital equipment, i.e. data on extending shift working in industry. The fact is that the gradual mobilization of such reserves provides a factor of steady growth and fails to explain deceleration.

The view that the said reserves were exhausted around 1960 (leading to the conclusion that the latent conflict between "extensive" development and restricted material and manpower resources therefore came out into the open in the following years) is true only for a limited area, perhaps for some consumer industries, or in the infrastructure where the theory of "big push"[3] applies. The new management system, if it is consistently implemented, will undoubtedly reveal good prospects even in sectors where reserves seem to be exhausted. True, as in the other older industrial countries, some natural and other resources are being gradually drained — e.g. traditional resource of power, ores, ferrous and non-ferrous metals etc.[4]

For the question under consideration, eliminating or severely restricting the "inflationary" effect of the gross output indicator is also a secondary matter. According to estimates available,[5] the distortion amounted to about one per cent at growth rates of 15—20 per cent, and was almost negligible in the second half of the fifties. Therefore, even with the inflationary effect

---

[3]  P. N. ROSENSTEIN-RODAN, *Notes on the Theory of Big Push in Economic Development of Latin America*, New York 1961, pp. 57—81.

[4]  See FLEK, KRUŽÍK, LEVČÍK, *Ekonomické soutěžení mezi kapitalismem a socialismem* (Economic Competition Between Capitalism and Socialism), Prague 1961, pp. 59—60.

[5]  G. J. STALLER, "Czechoslovak Industrial Growth", 1948—59, *American Economic Review*, 3/52/1962, pp. 385—407.

of the given indicator completely excluded, the resultant connection would be merely about 0·1 per cent a year over about ten years.

In its original application to capitalist development, the theory of stagnation explains loss of dynamism that in reality was a product of the given production relations and the alleged maturity of advanced capitalist economies. Non-Marxist economists such as J. A. Schumpeter[6] have pointed out that it originated as an attempt at whitewashing during the great depression, and in the postwar even its creators foresook it, switching over from "stagnation" to questions of economic growth. Therefore the effort to sell a "dead duck" from capitalist economic theory as an instrument for analysing socialist dynamics[7] holds out little promise. After all, the deceleration effects that undoubtedly operate in the socialist countries concerned are not inherent to their social order.

We have seen, then, that loss of tempo cannot be explained by the above factors. We shall show below, in agreement with other analysis,[8] that it is an inevitable outcome of a conflict within the new social order, which can be overcome — that is, the conflict between the given model of planned management of the socialist economy and the conditions under which it operates at the time.

## Adequacy of the traditional system of planned management in the phase of socialist industrialization

As has been shown elsewhere,[9] the traditional system originated in the Soviet Union in circumstances that provided the soil for centralistic tendencies; these factors were the need for maximum growth rates and rapid structural change, a reserve of manpower and capacities, and a shortage of executive personnel. To a greater or lesser extent these factors were operative

[6]  JOSEPH A. SCHUMPETER, *History of Economic Analysis*, London 1955, p. 1172.
[7]  G. WARREN NUTTER, "Some Observations on Soviet Industrial Growth", *American Economic Review*, 2/1957.
[8]  OTA ŠIK, *Příspěvek k analýze našeho hospodářského rozvoje* (Contribution to Analysis of Our Economic Development), Research publication, Institute of Economics CAS, 5/1965, and analysis by the Planning Commission for 1965.
[9]  W. Brus, Ogólne problemy funkcjonowania gospodarki socjalistycznej, Warsaw 1961, pp. 147—151, 331—332

in the countries with which we are concerned, at the start of their socialist industrialization. (The manpower shortage of those days in Czechoslovakia, which has been the subject of so much discussion, was later seen to be more of a specific shortfall in some sectors than a general shortage — the labour force rose by 400,000 between 1948 and 1955).

Centralistic management enabled large investment funds to be assembled and used at key points. By selective operation, and assigning highly detailed plan targets from the centre, it was able to clear the many bottlenecks that were bound to appear during rapid growth. A further argument in its favour was the lack of specialist and politically trained personnel who might have been entrusted with wider areas of economic decision-making.

The advantages of this system therefore outweighed its disadvantages, which incidentally did not play so big a part at the time as later. For instance, technological advance and production effectiveness were not yet foremost considerations, because rapid growth could be generated from reserves even with the given level of technology and effectiveness. Moreover, the situation on the home and foreign markets was exceptionally favourable for sales.

## *Origin of contradiction between the productive forces and the traditional system*

The well-known shortcomings in the traditional system of planning and management, including the high degree of monopolization, exert a much stronger retarding influence than in the early stages of planned economy. The higher the economic level, the more varied is the pattern of final and intermediate consumption, and the more complicated the process of socialist reproduction; and, consequently, the more imperfect are all attempts to comprehend and direct the process by means of systems employing volume indicators assigned from the top, and all the other traditional instruments of planning. A developed economy is, therefore, susceptible to the fact that the said system allows, indeed encourages, production of commodities without an ensured market, with a resultant piling up of inventories throughout the economy, which is hard to stop. What is more, the other negative feature of the system (whether they concern investment construction, technological development or effectiveness of production) have a much wider range of action today and are much more dangerous than they were at the time of socialist industrialization.

This is, then, a clear case of an out-dated management system holding back the advance of production relations and causing them to lag behind the growing productive forces. In these circumstances it was essential to put an end to the still widespread idea that the centralized model was somehow sanctified as an achievement of the socialist revolution, and was the sole possible type of planned management, while the decentralized model would, allegedly, imply a return to capitalist methods. On the contrary, a further deepening of the social quality in ownership of the means of production paves the way to a sharper divergence of the two social systems and not to a convergence, as is sometimes proclaimed by the sensation-mongers in some Western newspapers.

As for the alleged contradiction between plan and market, the question appears to have been answered already. It was theoretically elucidated — of course, with reference to the situation of the day — in the remarkable Soviet discussions of the twenties, which to the grave detriment of economic theory and practice were suddenly extinguished in the days of the "cult".

From the empirical standpoint an answer to the question of this alleged plan-market split may perhaps be provided by fuller examination of the decentralized model in Yugoslavia, which has been operating for fifteen years and showing on the whole successful planned development with persistently high growth rates.

## b) Leakages in the formation and distribution of the national income

We can therefore eliminate from the factors that might explain the gradual loss of dynamism the alleged maturity of the economy, and the supposed distorting effect of the gross output index. The causal relation between exhaustion of reserves through socialist reconstruction and the deceleration also seems to be of limited significance.

Statistical material available for three of the four countries concerned allows for a fairly reliable isolation of the economic processes accompanying — or more exactly, conditioning — the long-term slow-down. They give an answer (though with some reservations) to the question why the long-term quite high share of accumulation and the considerable lead held by production of capital goods over consumer goods failed to accelerate growth, but on the contrary produced quite strong deceleration. What happened to the equipment and materials destined, certainly in adequate quantities, for the purposes of expanded reproduction? Experience indicates that accumulation is not necessarily effective. (This is especially true in regard to relative growth of inventories or of capital-under-construction). Further, the combination of factors of production has not always been chosen suitably, because there was a failure to achieve rational minimization of the ratio between the inputs of material and human resources and the results gained from the production process. The figures in Table 4 give an interesting, though approximate, picture of the two main channels by which a growing proportion of the total social product escapes from the reproduction process. For discussion of the third, i.e. the unfavourable trend of the input—output relation, see Chapter V.

**Table 4** *in 1,000 mil. crowns*

| Czechoslovakia | 1956 | 1957 | 1958 | 1959 | 1960 | 1961 | 1962 | 1963 | 1964 | 1965 |
|---|---|---|---|---|---|---|---|---|---|---|
| Increment in inventories | 3 | 1 | 4 | 1 | 5 | 9 | 9 | 6 | — | . |
| Increment in capital-under-construction | 3 | 4 | 7 | 4 | 1 | 10 | 9 | −1 | −4 | . |
| Total accumulation | 16 | 21 | 26 | 27 | 28 | 35 | 32 | 22 | 17 | 15 |
| National income formed | 133 | 141 | 149 | 152 | 163 | 172 | 175 | 173 | 170 | 174 |

**Source:** To 1960, *Plánované hospodářství* (1964) no. 11; from *Ekonomický časopis* (1966) no. 4; current prices.

The table shows that a large part of accumulation — close on a third over the years stated — was tied down in inventories and capital-under-construction, the volume of which (in 1963 some 100,000 million crowns in inventories and 40,000 millions in capital-under-construction) was criticized at the start of the period under consideration. (Primarily the national income, as a source of accumulation and nonproductive consumption, was reduced in comparison with the level it could have reached if the input — output ratio in production had shown optimal development).

The favourable inventory trend in 1964 and 1965 corresponds in its causes and extent with the similar development at the time of deceleration in 1953 – 4. It, therefore, signifies no radical change. But we cannot exclude the possibility that anticipation of the good effects of the new economic system may have strengthened the favourable move in 1965.

## Poland

Only data on inventory growth are available for Poland. The growth in capital-under-construction is included in the available statistical sources under accumulation flowing to capital assets (see Table 5).

**Table 5**

| Poland | 1956 | 1957 | 1958 | 1959 | 1960 | 1961 | 1962 | 1963 | 1964 |
|---|---|---|---|---|---|---|---|---|---|
| Increment in inventories | 14 | 26 | 24 | 21 | 27 | 32 | 31 | 34 | 36 |
| Total accumulation | 51 | 74 | 78 | 87 | 90 | 102 | 101 | 113 | 120 |
| National income formed | 257 | 301 | 321 | 346 | 375 | 411 | 426 | 460 | 497 |

Source: *Rocznik statystyczny* 1957, 1960, 1963, 1965.
       1,000 million zloty at current prices.

Comparison of the figures for inventory trends in Poland and Czechoslovakia shows that in Poland, over 28 per cent of accumulation was tied in inventories alone over the period concerned. Comparison of data on inventories in Czechoslovakia with the corresponding figures for Hungary is also interesting (see Table 6).

**Table 6**

| Hungary | 1955 | 1956 | 1957 | 1958 | 1959 | 1960 | 1961 | 1962* | 1963* | 1964* |
|---|---|---|---|---|---|---|---|---|---|---|
| Growth of inventories | 8·9 | −5·5 | 16·9 | 4·4 | 8·0 | 9·5 | 13·1 | 16·3 | 17·6 | 17·9 |
| Growth in capital-under-construction | 0·5 | 1·3 | 0·3 | 0·6 | 10·0 | 2·0 | 1·4 | | | |
| Accumulation | 19·1 | 3·5 | 26·1 | 15·9 | 27·3 | 35·9 | 37·5 | 42·0 | 46·4 | 49·3 |

* Estimate according to Economic Survey of Europe, tab. 1.
**Source:** UNO-EEC 1962, Geneva 1963. (*Economic Survey for Europe*)
1,000 million forint.

## Hungary

In Hungary, too, inventory expansion for the period concerned amounts on average to over one-third of total accumulation and the sum of increments in inventories and capital-under-construction to nearly 35 per cent. The bigger annual fluctuations in inventory growth − compared with Czechoslovakia − can evidently be explained by the events of 1956 and the compensatory movement in the following year; recent years, however, show a tendency towards lasting growth in inventories, as in Czechoslovakia. But the increments in capital-under-construction are much less in Hungary.

## German Democratic Republic

Time series are not available here.
There are, however, figures for the level of capital-under-construction and inventories in one year, and these are comparable with the corresponding figures for the other countries (see Table 7).
The fact emerges that the overall volume of assets tied down in investment projects in progress is highest in Czechoslovakia and the GDR. In these countries it reaches about one-fifth or more of the national income

**Table 7.** *Volume of capital-under-construction (1962)*

| Country | National income | Investments | Capital-under-construction at end of year | | |
|---|---|---|---|---|---|
| | | | in 1,000 millions | in % of annual investments | in % of national income |
| Czechoslovakia | 172 | 37 | 40 | 108 | 22 |
| Poland | 443 | 124 | 75 | 60 | 17 |
| Hungary | 147 | 37 | 51 | 72 | 13 |
| GDR | 77 | 16 | 15 | 97 | 19 |

Source: Official data of UNO-EEC, Geneva 1963.

and roughly equals the annual total of investment expenditure. The situation in Poland and Hungary is somewhat better, but in Hungary the proportion of capital-under-construction to the national income is more marked.

## Some capitalist countries

Table 8 shows the rather high share of inventory expansion in the national income compared with some capitalist countries. The comparison

**Table 8.** *Increments in inventories in 1960 as proportion of national income*

| | % | | % |
|---|---|---|---|
| Czechoslovakia | 4·5 | Great Britain | 3·8 |
| Poland | 6·9 | France | 2·9 |
| Hungary | 5·2 | Italy | 2·5 |
| GDR | 5·8 | Belgium | 1·0 |

Sources: Official publications cited from UNO, Economic Survey for Europe, 1962, pp. 1—31; *Rudé právo* of Jan. 30, 1963.
Note: Czechoslovakia for 1963, GDR for 1958.

was made on the basis of an identical definition of national income (To some extent, however, the data for inventories in the socialist countries include items that are not covered, or only partially covered, by statistics from the capitalist countries).

## Results of analysis of leakages

If we take the data for Czechoslovakia, Poland, and Hungary as more or less representative of all the countries in question, we may estimate that the share of accumulation in circulating assets (i.e. inventories) amounts on average to about one-third of total accumulation. With the (total) rate of accumulation at 12−18 per cent, accumulation in circulating assets amounts to 4−6 per cent of the national income.

We can see from the time series for Czechoslovakia and Hungary that accumulation in capital under construction represents about 10 per cent of total accumulation, that is 1·2 to 1·8 per cent of the national income formed. Partial data for the other countries indicate that this share is fairly typical for the group of countries concerned.

In fact, increments in inventories and capital under construction in these countries tie down an appreciable, indeed the greater part, of increments in the national income. This means a considerable reduction in the increments available for raising consumption or for accumulation in capital projects[10] put into operation.

In addition, we shall try in a later chapter to demonstrate that increments in national income are increasingly influenced by the somewhat unfavourable trend in the ratio of production inputs to performance measured by final products.

There is no great difficulty in making an approximate computation of how far growth in national income could be accelerated if inventories and capital under construction were at an essential minimum and were to rise more or less in line with growth of the national income. The growth of inventories and capital under construction, alongside the relatively unfavour-

[10] See also A. ZAUBERMANN, *Industrial Progress in Poland, Czechoslovakia and Eastern Germany 1937−1962*, London 1964, p. 51.

able trend of input—output in the production process, may be considered to be the immediate cause of the loss of dynamism.

## c) The basic cause of gradual loss of dynamics

Relationship between the structural and model factors in excessive growth of inventories and capital under construction and in the unfavourable input—output trend of the reproduction process.

After nearly twenty years of a planned economy, it is possible to include the sectoral and branch structures among the outcomes of the system of planning and management.[11] It can be demonstrated that development hitherto, for example of Czechoslovak industry towards an ineffective structure, has itself been induced by the traditional system of planning and management. As long as the central planners themselves stood on the platform of this system, they necessarily saw the almost chronic deficit in raw materials, power, materials and the like as a real deficit. From the angle of the traditional system, they were incapable of recognizing how it was conditioned by factors of the model. There was, therefore, no alternative but to expand capacities by heavy investment expenditure, which in the circumstances grew less and less effective.

Insofar as the view was voiced that it would be advantageous to put more into reconstructing existing capacities with the aim of cutting inputs and raising productivity, it naturally met with the argument that there was still plenty of scope for improvement with the existing standards of input and performance: the thing was to "mobilize" these reserves and not allow dispersion of investment means to minor projects that were really not particularly effective in the context of the centralized model. But in this context even such "mobilization" was not effective. In the tug of war among contradictory plan indicators it was the quantitative plan targets that in most cases won the day, being most closely allied to the material and moral incentives for groups and individuals.

---

[11] There is also autonomous decision-making by the supreme planning authorities, which operates as a relatively independent factor. The autonomy, and especially the extent of potential error, are in large measure determined by the given management model.

Consequently, the downward trend of the growth rate can only appear as the objective outcome of a single factor — the direct and indirect operation of the traditional management system.[12] But this discovery is not much help when we go beyond analysis of past development and start to look for and weigh up the possible ways of putting things right. To achieve this we need first of all to understand to what extent the long-term deceleration is due to the direct operation of the traditional system and to what extent it stems indirectly from the economic structure shaped by the said system.

The negative consequences deriving directly from the operation of the centralized model have already been the subject of much discussion. Therefore we will not here go into the oft-repeated disclosures of these now obvious shortcomings, but will concentrate on the quantitative analysis of their economic effects. Some classification is needed for such an attempt, and we have taken it from the work by W. Brus quoted above.[13]

1. Inflexibility of production, primarily in regard to adapting the product mix to the demands of customers, both in the spheres of production and consumption; unsatisfactory production quality linked with this.

2. Excessive unit inputs, especially of materials.

3. Insufficient incentive to technological development, both as to improving production methods and improving products.

4. Shortcomings and disharmony within the system of economic stimuli, which undermines any sense of interconnection among the interests of individuals, groups and society (problem of alienation).

5. Spread of bureaucracy in the government and economic administration.

And now we need to examine the relationship of these model factors — or some of them — to the leakages already dealt with in this chapter.

---

[12] The relation between the model of planning and management and Kalecki's growth model was analysed by Prof. W. Brus in a lecture delivered in Prague on September 29, 1964.

[13] W. Brus, ibid. pp. 154—156.

## Inflexibility of production in the centralized model and overgrowth of inventories

As mentioned above, the centralized model originated in the Soviet Union at a much lower level of economic development with a comparatively simple and stable structure of productive and nonproductive needs, and with a negligible share of export in the total outputs of sectors.

One of the inevitable consequences of operating the centralized model in the diametrically opposed conditions of a peace-time economy at a higher level of development, with the demands of productive and final consumption becoming increasingly varied and fluid and with the international division of labour assuming growing importance, has already been recorded in the tables — that is, the expansion of inventories. The leakage resulting from the high share of inventory growth in the national income may be considered as a product of model (and not structural) factors.

The piling up of inventories is sometimes presented as a result of exceptional circumstances in recent years — delays in plan drafting and frequent changes. But the figures given are mainly for a year when conditions where fairly normal. This indicates that the difficulties of 1961–3 and their consequences were purely secondary factors in the overgrowth of inventories. The primary factor was the inflexibility inherent in the centralized model. In this model, the principle of planning is taken to signify that the central planning authority not only incorporates the leading macroeconomic decisions in the plan (rate of accumulation, distribution of investment assets, distribution of consumption assets, the main proportions of current production, the chief investment projects etc.), but in addition reserves to the area of central planning such matters as decisions on the volume and structure of production in individual enterprises, the amount and composition of costs, types of sales outlets and sources of supply. In principle, the only matters left outside the scope of central directive planning are micro-economic decisions, for instance on the individual consumption pattern for a given income level, and questions of choice of employment and place of work. (And even such decisions are often made centrally and directively).

Handing assigned targets down the line in the sphere of ordinary economic decision-making, however, implies a hierarchic dependence of the plans of lower links on those worked out by the superior organs. With the high degree of correlation among all economic processes, any change of plan within the centralized model is, therefore, bound to involve discussion at the level of ministries, contacts between ministries, and possibly at the level of the government and its specialist bodies. Of course, all this requires time — the more time, the more overloaded the superior authorities become and the more the centralized model inevitably runs counter to the well-known principle valid for every system of management, that of pyramiding decisions. *De minimis non curat praetor* was the principle of administration recognized by the Romans. But two thousand years after we are apt to forget it (in fact, under the given system of management, we were forced to forget it).

Time is not halted by inter-ministry discussions, and production goes ahead. So we get an accumulation of stocks for which there is no assured outlet, and they include capital goods, which thereby provide a demonstration of their commodity nature even under socialism. Alternatively, production of a "debatable" line is temporarily halted, and then inventories pile up in the hands of suppliers. The various agencies involved in the case are then joined — in an unenviable role — by the arbitrator.

These complications engendered by the rigidity of the centralized model are the more serious, because under certain circumstances they may pave the way to a chain reaction throughout the economy. When the centre is overloaded with disputable cases of day-to-day decision-making, there are bound to be break-downs in the reproduction process; the need to cope with them adds to the burden of the centre, and so on.

The trend of inventories is aggravated by what is known as "speculation in a socialist economy". Since, under the centralized model, supplies are channeled to enterprises by detailed directions of the plan, a phase of intensified disequilibrium and failure to fulfill production plans may lead to redoubled efforts to step up material inputs etc. It should be understood that an enterprise does not order materials according to its financial resources earned by sales of its products, but on a broad basis of its original allocation determined by the plan balance, within the scope of which its claims for materials are the larger the shorter the supplies available.

This explains why at a time when, for objective reasons stated in the previous chapter, the main disproportions have been overcome and supplies are smoother, the subjective propensity to hoard inventories, overstate requirements of materials and so on (and to "grab" new investment projects) is weaker. In years of extreme economic tension, general shortages and acute imbalance between supply and demand, they are far stronger. In a situation such as that of 1961−3, the shortcomings of planning and management could, therefore, induce such a strong chain reaction throughout the economy − with an impact abroad, too.

## Inflexibility of production in the centralized model and overgrowth of capital-under-construction

The survey of capital-under-construction suggests that this disease, too, is not specifically Czechoslovak, but that in socialist countries operating the centralized model it has assumed epidemic proportions.

The causes usually advanced − monotonously for over fifteen years − are lack of discipline among investors, inadequate preparation of projects and non-fulfilment of deadlines by sub-contractors. Probably in any socialist economic model it would be fairly difficult to carry out extensive investment programmes at high growth rates and with scanty or non-existent reserves of productive capacity. But the almost chronic failure to keep to time schedules in the building industry, in engineering and design organizations, evidently stems from the contrast between the inherently inflexible centralized model (suited to fairly stable and uniform needs in the productive and nonproductive spheres), and the completely different conditions existing in these sectors especially. The question of "lack of discipline among investors" has been referred to above. In fact, the leakage incurred by freezing resources in capital-under-construction can also be put at the door of direct influence exerted by model factors.

## Excessive unit inputs in the centralized model

To find the causes of the unfavourable trend between production inputs and performance is more difficult than in the case of the first two leakages. (For more detailed treatment, see the next chapter). Undoubtedly, the tying of incentives to volume indicators encourages enterprises and individuals to maximize output rather than minimize input.[14] The prime cause of the relative decline in effectiveness of the reproduction process is not, therefore, in the economic structure shaped by the macroeconomic, "extensive" development that has been followed, but would seem to lie in the ineffective utilization of the factors of production at different levels. Just as the traditional system operated ineffectively and deformed the input structure at the microeconomic level (enterprises and plants), it has also operated ineffectively at the macroeconomic level and has deformed the sectoral and branch structure of the economy.

Here again, the leakage cannot be ascribed to macroeconomic factors — the structural trend in sectors and branches — in the first place. The high inputs of materials, labour and capital, for example, in Czechoslovak industry, is in reality a product of microeconomic factors — the long-term operation of the centralized model at the enterprise and plant level. It stems from the fact that economic calculation, which is a powerful instrument of rational operation, was converted by degrees into a formal version of "*khozraschot*", with a negligible effect on economic processes.

From an examination of the extent and main causes of the three leakages, we may draw the following conclusion. Long-term deceleration is primarily a direct outcome of the traditional system of planning and management. Only to a much lesser degree is the downturn in the growth rate an indirect product of the traditional system by way of the economic structure shaped by this system.


*Consequences of insufficient incentive to technological development*

The correlation between the traditional system and technological development is perhaps best stated by Prof. Brus.[15] In fact, the common formulation of the problem, which has been adopted in the heading of this passage, is, to say the least, inaccurate. The issue is not really that of insuffi-

---

[14] Their interest is directed to quantitative targets at the expense of qualitative.
[15] W. Brus, ibid., pp. 205—206.

cient incentive to technological development, but of strong counter-incentives built into the system.

The effectiveness of technological development is an economic category that is exceptionally difficult to quantify. One has the impression that the best approach will be to concentrate on the microeconomic level, with representative surveys in selected works. Nevertheless, even the mass of partial information that is available is sufficiently significant to confirm the decelerating effect of the traditional system on technological development.

### Other economic consequences of the centralized model

As for the remaining shortcomings in the traditional system, as listed according to Prof. Brus's classification in the introduction to this chapter, their effects on the level reached by the economy and the growth rate, although qualitatively indubitable, cannot be isolated and quantified by a direct method. Naturally, it is obvious that the economic consequences of alienation and bureaucracy are evinced in a slowing down of growth in productivity, reducing the effectiveness of investments and hampering technological progress (and in the resultant drop in the growth rate). There seems to be little doubt that the sinking trend of the growth rate and its effect on living standards, together with the two factors, examined here, which contribute to this negative trend and are reinforced by its echo-effect, carry more than economic implication.

## d) Outcome of discussion of long-term changes in the rate of growth

### Overgrowth of inventories and of capital-under-construction

Discussion following the publication of articles on short- and long-term changes in the growth rate has confirmed one of the main conclusions, namely that the long-term growth of inventories and capital-under-construction (proportionate to growth in national income) in the countries under consideration is sufficiently significant to be regarded as one of the immediate causes of the deceleration observed in the long-term rate of growth. Nor can there be any doubt about the further conclusion that both decelerators — overgrowth of inventories and of capital-under-construction — are themselves conditioned by the traditional model of planning and management.

## Materials inputs

While the discussion has not, at least so far, involved any substantial modification in the analysis of the two leakages mentioned above, this is not the case for the leakage defined as relative increase in materials inputs to production. As already stated in an article on deceleration of the growth rate,[16] to total the detailed quantitative results obtained would "require further research, primarily as to the influence of structural factors on the trends of the leakages, especially on the relative growth of materials inputs." Contributions to discussion by Mačica and V. Nachtigal[17] have thrown further light on this problem and opened up a new approach to the analysis.

While statistical elimination of the influence of structural changes on the (relative) level of materials inputs has yielded a result similar to that of the original investigation, this was the case only insofar as the analysis was confined to structural changes involving broad economic sectors (mining and manufacturing, building, agriculture etc.). A more detailed analysis gave a different picture. The fact is that if statistical data are freed of the influence exerted by structural changes within industry, i.e. by sectors, and if the distorting effect produced by the differentiated impact of the turnover tax[18] is also eliminated, relative materials inputs are found to have been more or less stable up to 1960, with an upward turn later.

This result calls for two comments. In the first place, it is, like our

---

[16] *Plánované hospodářství*, 11/1964, p. 27.

[17] *Plánované hospodářství*, 2 and 4/1965.

[18] V. NACHTIGAL, *Statistika*, 12/1965. The differentiated impact of the turnover tax appears to boost materials inputs because the tax burden falls mainly on products in group B, which has a lower growth rate combined with a larger share of the net product. On the other hand, group A, which shows more rapid growth, records a smaller share in the net product and hence a larger share in materials inputs.

original result, in sharp contrast to data available for industrially developed countries in the West. During the last two or three decades the relative consumption of materials in these countries has actually dropped considerably. According to Haberler's reports[19], in the period 1939–54, the proportion of natural raw materials inputs to total commodities output in western Europe, the US and Japan dropped from 17·8 per cent to 13·3 per cent. An extremely interesting piece of work by the Hungarian economist Ferencz Jánossy, with the cooperation of E. Ehrlich, has yielded a similar result using an original method. It shows that in Czechoslovakia and Hungary the tendency is for consumption per head of population to be higher in the case of power, raw materials and materials, and lower for final products, than in capitalist countries with comparable levels of national income. The conclusion to be drawn is that the relative stability of materials inputs in Czechoslovakia in 1955–60 still does not point to optimal development, irrespective of the fact that they are evidently higher than in advanced capitalist countries. Therefore, it is still true that this leakage is present and is depressing the potential growth of the Czechoslovak economy compared with the above-mentioned countries.

The second comment on the outcome of the discussion refers to the fact that the relative rise in real production costs, including not only materials, but also labour and capital assets, can be documented by another method described in Chapter V. And in general it seems that to take materials inputs in isolation from the trends of other factors is in itself a relic of the past, just another example of outdated thinking. From the angle of rational operation, the point is not whether materials inputs go up, down or stay the same. In reality the factors of production are always being interchanged. The job of an enterprise is to operate rationally and, by means of economic calculations, to determine the optimal combination of production factors, of the substitutions that will lead to optimal combination when total inputs are minimised. This is the theoretical reason leading us to choose a different approach than that employed in the work published in *Plánované hospodářství*[20]. (See the following chapter).

---

[19] *Trends in International Trade*, Geneva 1958, p. 40.

[20] *Plánované hospodářství*, no. 11/1964.

Chapter V.

# Trend in the Relation of Domestic and World Prices, and Production Costs*

"World trade is the vital condition of the world economy and social progress. It is an essential condition of progress, the *conditio sine qua non* at the moment when we are starting to write a new page in the history of mankind..."

RAGNAR FRISCH

## a)   Grounds for the method of analysis proposed

The growing disparity between the level of domestic and world prices is of such long standing in Czechoslovakia (and not only there) that economists have come to look at it as more or less a fact of nature. Although this disparity stems from vital economic processes affecting the very groundwork of the economy, no examination has been made of its origin, or of the factors shaping its development hitherto. Protection of the home price system from the fluctuations of world markets was unequivocally and unreservedly proclaimed as one of the prime advantages of the traditional administrative directive system of planning and management.

In examining the effectiveness of foreign trade, prior attention was directed to its development at the microeconomic level, mainly for the operative purposes of determining the advantages of exporting (or importing) various types or groups of commodities. Such methods are more suited to discovering the relative advantageousness of exporting one or another type of product from the angle of foreign currency returns than to revealing the general and underlying causes of a widening price gap. The phenomena signalized by this divergence of domestic and world prices therefore remained outside the field of economic investigation.

In contrast, surveys of the macroeconomic effectiveness of the Czechoslovak economy have so far been conducted mainly on the basis of analysis

* This chapter has been written in collaboration with Mr. Jan Pleva.

83

of productivity dynamics, effectiveness of fixed assets and the trend of material inputs. But this method can usually be employed solely for investigating development in time, that is for development trends. International comparisons of this type are far from easy and, as a rule, the results are not satisfactory.

A further disadvantage of the method is that it is confined to following how individual production factors are utilized in isolation from the others, without a synthetic picture of their effectiveness in their theoretically optimal combination. Changes and the rates of change in the overall effectiveness of the economy can, however, be determined solely through complex observation of (mutually interchangeable) production factors, i.e. through examining aggregate costs in relation to total earnings.

The difficulty in distinguishing between profitability achieved by minimizing unit costs of material and labour, and that achieved by open and concealed price adjustments, signifies that even observation of the profitability trend fails to give a correct picture of the overall development of effectiveness in the economy.[1] On the assumption (which in fact is only roughly true, and only in larger aggregation) that price movements reflect the dynamics of production costs, the gap between world and domestic price trends should signalize divergences in the trend of production costs. In view of the high share of export in total production and its rather stable structure, price and cost changes for the export component of industrial output can be taken as representative for industrial output as a whole. This would enable the development of factor input per unit of output − i.e. of real costs in Czechoslovakia to be assessed as follows.

The best approach would be to limit this investigation to export to capitalist markets, where prices are essentially objective, being shaped in the long term by the movements of costs among the chief world producers.[2] Their trend could, therefore, serve as a base for comparison in assessing the movement of Czechoslovak domestic prices, (and real costs), which, as is the case in other socialist countries, are more strongly affected by subjective decisions. But the statistical material published, only enables us to

---

[1] This is fully confirmed by results obtained by the State Planning Commission (1965) in analysing the development of the Czechoslovak economy.

[2] For the influence of inflationary tendencies on world markets, see below.

**Table 9.** *Trend of the relation between domestic and world price levels (Czechoslovak industrial export, 1955–64).*

| | | 1955 | 1956 | 1957 | 1958 | 1959 | 1960 | 1961 | 1962 | 1963 | 1964 |
|---|---|---|---|---|---|---|---|---|---|---|---|
| 1. Industrial output at selling prices | 1,000 mil. Kčs | 158·6 | 169·2 | 181·0 | 195·4 | 206·9 | 223·3 | 242·2 | 257·1 | 257·9 | 262·7 |
| 2. Share of turnover tax | per cent | 24·4 | 21·9 | 20·6 | 20·8 | 18·3 | 15·8 | 19·7 | 16·5 | 16·6 | 15·6 |
| 3. Industrial output net of turnover tax | 1,000 mil. Kčs | 119·9 | 132·1 | 143·7 | 154·8 | 169·0 | 188·0 | 194·5 | 214·7 | 215·1 | 221·7 |
| 4. Share of export in industrial output | per cent | 10·2 | 11·5 | 11·0 | 11·0 | 12·4 | 13·4 | 13·8 | 14·0 | 15·6 | 15·6 |
| 5. Export of industrial products at domestic prices (net of turnover tax) | 1,000 mil. Kčs | 12·23 | 15·19 | 15·81 | 17·03 | 20·96 | 25·19 | 26·84 | 30·06 | 33·56 | 34·59 |
| 6. Export of industrial products at world prices | 1,000 mil. Kčs | 7·75 | 9·00 | 8·85 | 10·04 | 11·45 | 12·91 | 13·57 | 14·75 | 16·55 | 17·35 |
| 7. Ratio of domestic to world prices | | | | | | | | | | | |
| a) foreign prices = 100% | 1,000 mil. Kčs | 157·8 | 168·8 | 178·6 | 169·6 | 183·1 | 195·1 | 197·8 | 203·8 | 202·8 | 199·4 |
| b) domestic prices = 100% | | 63·4 | 59·2 | 56·0 | 59·0 | 54·6 | 51·2 | 50·6 | 49·1 | 49·3 | 50·2 |

**Sources and notes:**

1. Statistical yearbook 1965, p. 135; Social product created in industry (at current prices).
2. Statistical yearbook 1965, p. 181, and earlier yearbooks: Sales structure of goods-producing industries.
3. Estimates by formula: (3) = (1) − [(1) . (2)]/100.
4. Statistical yearbook 1965, p. 384, and earlier yearbooks: Share of export in industrial production.
5. Estimates by formula: (5) = [(3) . (4)]/100.
6. Statistical yearbook 1965, p. 383, and earlier yearbooks: Export by commodity groups — items I, IIa—c, IVb, V.
7. a) By formula (5)/(6).
   b) By formula (6)/(5).

follow the general trend of price and real costs disparity, relative to the world market as a whole. We therefore chose the procedure indicated in in table No. 9.

Of course, difficulties arise with the influence of currency factors, the specific features of price formation in Czechoslovakia, and so on. Nevertheless, the advantage of a fairly objective yardstick such as the prices actually commanded by exporting enterprises on world markets, compared with the difficulty in interpreting other statistical data (especially figures derived from gross output) does perhaps justify the attempt to find such a new approach.

b)  Trend in the relation of domestic and world
    price levels

Table 9 surveys the changing relation between world and domestic prices as an indicator of the relative trend in real costs. It comprises data for exports of Czechoslovak manufactures according to the Czechoslovak statistical yearbook. From this approximation we see that in 1955 foreign trade enterprises earned in Czechoslovak crowns at foreign exchange parity about 63 per cent of the amount paid out at domestic prices to Czechoslovak producers for export goods. The table further shows that by 1964 this percentage had dropped to about 50. This signifies that in 1955 the domestic price level was roughly 58 per cent higher $(100/63 = 1·58)$ and in 1963 twice as high $(100/50 \cong 2)$ as the price level on world markets.

The computation had to work with the figures available. Therefore, as seen in the table, our estimate covers industrial production at final selling prices in the case of consumer goods, including the retail trade mark-up. The share of export, on the other hand, is recorded in the statistics industrial output in our definition, but on a gross output basis. While these and other inaccuracies affect the results for a given year, they do not exclude chronological comparison. In analysing time series, the statistical errors are almost entirely compensated.

Up to 1948, however, when the monopoly foreign trade organizations were set up and the so-called equalizing fund was introduced, no disparity actually existed. Export enterprises purchased on the home market at current prices and usually marketed abroad at a profit. Examination of how the gap arose shows that it can be ascribed to three factors, of which two have no direct economic effect, while the third is immediately relevant to the question of economic effectiveness in Czechoslovakia.

## Czechoslovak currency revaluation in 1953

A technical cause of the relative rise in domestic prices (which in itself has no economic significance) can be found in part in the revaluation of the Czechoslovak crown in 1953. The gold content of the currency unit was raised so that the exchange rate of the dollar changed from 10 Czechoslovak crowns to 7·20 crowns. Czechoslovak domestic prices rose by 39 per cent against world prices. The resultant export losses were, of course, balanced by a corresponding gain on imports.

## Currency trend, 1948—53

The second factor underlying the price gap, which is also neutral with respect to the long-term effectiveness of the economy, was the currency trend in 1948—53. This was a period of rapid structural change, a sharp rise in employment and an appreciable advance in average nominal incomes, generating a rapid expansion of purchasing power. But under the circumstances this growth was far from being balanced by a corresponding advance in supplies of consumer goods and services. The outcome was a gradual rise in prices, culminating in an across-the-board price adjustment.

Figures for the trend of the social product at current and constant prices through 1948—53[3] indicate that the price level rose by about 30 per cent. But the price index obtained in this way is mixed, because it includes private consumption at retail prices, public consumption and accumulation at wholesale prices. Since the rise in retail prices was well above the advance in the overall price level (given by the said index), one has to assume that

---

[3] See *Czechoslovak Statistical Abstract 1965*, pp. 135—136.

the wholesale price rise was less. For our purposes we may put it at not over 20 per cent.[4]

The joint influence exerted by revaluation and the currency trend in the above period on the relative rise in domestic wholesale prices against world prices (which we, in the meantime, take as a constant) can now be expressed by an index of 1·67 (1·39 × 1·20). It is necessary to explain a further relative rise in domestic wholesale prices, expressed by the ratio of index 1·67 and index 1·99, as seen in Table 9. That is, the rise is 1·67 : 1·99, i.e. 19 per cent.

## Relative rise in real production costs

All the indications are that this widening of the gap sprang from quite different causes than those operating in 1948 – 53. The retail price index for 1953 – 62 tended to sink and wage costs per unit of output were also more on the downgrade. Although in this period, too, concealed inflation pressures were manifested in varying intensities and extent, especially in the area of capital construction, it looks as if the further relative rise in domestic prices cannot be explained merely by monetary factors.

As a working hypothesis we may take the view that, on the contrary, the widening of the gap in the ratio of 1·67 to 1·99, i.e. by 19 per cent, expresses real changes in production costs[5] in relation to the costs recorded by the chief world exporters. Indeed, it is not out of the question that a similar tendency started to operate in the period up to 1953.

In this connection we employ the concept of disparity in prices and production costs always in respect of comparable use value. For example, the fact that Czechoslovak machinery can command on West European markets in general under two-thirds of the per-kilogramme prices attained by capitalist competitors, although the factor inputs for the Czechoslovak

---

[4]  See Č. KožušnÍk, *Problémy teorie hodnoty a ceny za socialismu* (Theory of Value and Prices under Socialism), NČSAV, Prague 1964, pp. 91—115. In view of the mixed type of price index employed here, its trend is also affected by a shift of emphasis from direct to indirect taxation made in the early fifties. Changes in proportion between production of producer and consumer goods also had an effect. In the first approximation we ignore both these factors.

[5]  Č. KožušnÍk, ibid. p. 153.

goods are often higher, is due to a lower technological level, inferior quality in the widest sense, inadequate equipment and servicing etc. Czechoslovak products, which in the past had a reputation for taste and quality, today tend to appear, especially on Western markets, as subsidiary assortment tending to the lower quality, and hence price, categories. The fact has to be faced that the existing level of quality can hardly be expected to maintain a lasting position even on the socialist market. Widening of the price gap is also aggravated by lack of agility on the part of commercial organizations, and also by some Eastern trade policies and Western customs barriers.

If we put aside the assumption made hitherto about the stability of world prices, we find that the relative rise of (real) production costs was still higher than indicated above.

In the 1955–63 period, the world price index for industiral products went up, according to UNO statistics, from 94 to 103. Consequently, the rise in domestic prices related to world prices is 30 per cent, not 19 (i.e. the index 119 goes up in the ratio 94 : 103 to 130).

c) Production costs and the centralized model. Elimination of the market mechanism and decline in rational operation

Empirical data having indicated that the growing gap between world and domestic price levels cannot be attributed purely to currency factors, but also – most clearly after 1953 – to a kind of cost inflation, there must be some underlying causes that have induced and encouraged this process.

With the change-over to a fully centralized, administrative method of planning and management, the goals assigned to enterprises were radically altered. The leading criterion became the quantitative indicator of gross output, while costs expended on production took second place. The principle of ecomic rationality was subordinated to the supreme goal of fulfilling and overfilling quantitative targets. The responsibility of an enterprise to keep a constant watch on costs and earnings, and to maximize profit, receded into the background. The main yardstick of performance came to be a mechanical comparison of output with the targets assigned by the plan from the top.

Such conditions provided a direct impulse to deterioration on the production costs front. Up to 1953, their relative increase was masked by a movement of the price level caused by the above-mentioned currency factors. But in the following period the currency effects receded and the continuing rise of domestic prices above world prices, induced by costs factors, became quite obvious.

So the loss of relative effectiveness indicated by the unsatisfactory trend of production costs appears as an inevitable consequence of eliminating the market mechanism in a key area of the economy. Enterprises that were isolated from world development, as evinced on world markets, by the long-term operation of so-called fixed wholesale prices were not exposed to objective influences that would have tested the suitability, quality, technological level and efficiency of their performance. Indeed, the entire economy was isolated from world markets by a barrier of planned, more or less fixed domestic prices and the monopoly organization of foreign trade. Not only was economic pressure from outside prevented from making a direct impact on enterprises, but also producers had no access to information as to the selling prices of their products on foreign markets. In any case, such information could have played no part in decision-making by enterprises, because the system of management set a different succes indicators than would have been indicated by the world market.

Two objections can be made to the above analysis and the conclusions drawn. Firstly, it can be argued that the relative rise in domestic prices could be a result of changes in the territorial and commodity structure of Czechoslovak export, rather than the differentiated trend of costs. True, some such changes did occur. But they are evidently insufficient as a full explanation of the marked deterioration in the relation of world and domestic prices. Moreover, it would be wrong to exclude the influence of these structural changes, because the fact that Czechoslovak exporters were forced to turn to "worse markets" or to deal in less advantageous commodities (from the angle of world and domestic prices) is actually a sign of a decline in competitiveness and effectiveness in the Czechoslovak economy.

Secondly, it can be argued that, since competition on world markets is imperfect, supplementary export is subjected, even without structural changes, to something in the nature of a law of diminishing returns.[6] The

---

[6] M. KALECKI, ibid., pp. 64—65.

seemingly highly abstract argumentation presented by Kalecki in the work referred to is, in fact, intimately connected with the practical problems of the Polish long-term plan. In the specific conditions of Poland, where export has been concentrated largely on coal and meat products, the tendency towards a diminishing marginal effectiveness of export undoubtedly applies. That it does not have to apply to Czechoslovak conditions is evident from the fact that other countries with a similar economic structure and raw material situation as Czechoslovakia (Switzerland, Holland) have appreciably stepped up their industrial exports over recent decades, and without loss of effectiveness. (On the short-term foreign-trade barriers, see Chapter III.)

Chapter VI

# Application of the Kalecki Model*

"An economist should not rely merely on recasting published sources, but should draw on the facts and data of living reality. An economist must be able to tune the mechanism of directing social production and regulate the operation of this mechanism."

V. S. NEMCHINOV

## a) Research project, theoretical and practical value

The present chapter links up with the results given in the foregoing chapters from the investigation of short- and long-term changes in the rate of growth. Its subject comprises analysis of correlations among the main parameters of the growth model on the one hand, and the effectiveness of the traditional model of socialist economic operation under changing circumstances on the other. Analysis of the correlation between the growth model and the model of economic operation is based on an attempt to apply Kalecki's model of economic growth under socialism to Czechoslovak empirical data for the 1950–65 period. By giving statistical content to the growth model it is hoped to provide a criterion of effectiveness for the system of planning and management at different levels of economic development.

### Parameters of the growth model and the system of planning and management

Research in Poland, Czechoslovakia and Yugoslavia has shown that the relations of production in the wider sense, that is including the given system of economic planning and management, have an influence on the strategic parameters of the growth model. The difference between the techno-

* The co-author of this chapter is Dr. Josef Flek/Kohn.

93

cratic and politico-economic approach both to economic analysis and to planning future economic development lies in this very question of the role assigned to the influence of production relations on growth parameters. Overlooking this influence is typical for planners of technocratic bent. Technocracy, which sees its machines alone, while ignoring the people behind them and their interests, is clearly a phenomenon that is independent of the given socio-economic formation. In Anglo-Saxon terminology the word growthmanship has come to be used for the technocratic conception whereby investment is the sole or predominant source of growth, while the active role of the human factor is overlooked or is even constrained by giving priority to accumulation at the expense of consumer interests.

Precise methods for empirical determination of the growth model parameters are still a matter of discussion. The subject is full of attraction for every economist, both in view of its key place in evaluation of past development, and of its importance for any forecasting of future growth. Preparatory work on drafting the long-term plan up to 1985 is largely concentrated on this point.

Both the methods employed for analysis and forecasting, and the results obtained for examining the long- and short-term changes in growth rate, may be something of a shock for economists accustomed to the usual text-book approach to the economic laws of socialism. Indeed, a few individuals have reacted in this way. Nevertheless, the gulf between economic theory and the actual job of socialist construction — a typical and frequently, but vainly, criticized feature of political economy in the thirties, forties and early fifties — seems impossible to bridge in any other way than by empirical research freed of many prejudices and *a priori* ideas about the results it should yield. The true test of the social usefulness of economic theory can lie solely in its effectiveness both in evaluating the past, and in tackling the problems of the present and immediate future. "There can be no dogmatism, where the greatest and sole criterion of doctrine is postulated as its concurrence with the actual process of socio-economic development."[1]

In the light of recent experience, however, we do not see this agreement as a mechanical accommodation of theory to the practical measures chosen, nor as a mere agreement of theoretical views with the superficial phenomenal

---

[1]  V. I. LENIN, *Works*, vol. 1, p. 311 (Czech edition).

forms of day-by-day economic life; we see it as cognition that is adequate to the inner tendencies in the movement of reality. Scientific cognition then implicitly includes a critical analysis of reality.

The problem of correlation between the leading parameters of the growth model and the overall effectiveness of the economy under changing conditions has not been posed for Czechoslovak economists purely by theory. It is also an urgent matter for practical planning. Taking into account the basic difficulties facing the Czechoslovak economy, especially industry, which stem primarily from the protracted operation of the old system of planning and management, and only in the second place form some structural disproportions, the dilemma for the planners can be formulated as follows:

How should a long-range plan that would employ the empirically determined parameters of the growth model be created when we know that these parameters have been modified, under the conditions operative hitherto, by the negative effects of the traditional model of operation? How is it possible to anticipate the positive effects flowing from transition to a decentralized model of management for a period that includes a stage of friction and painful adaptation?

In our view, the failure of some more long-term forecasts derives mainly from their authors' ignorance of this dilemma, or their lack of attention to it. This applies particularly to the first attempt at a hypothesis of long-term development dating from the late fifties, and in some measure to the third five-year plan for 1961 – 1965, because the procedure adopted by their authors was to all intents restricted to forecasting development by extrapolation of existing trends. But a more advanced stage of economic development presents snags capable of wrecking the extrapolation method. In the new conditions of economic growth such forecasts enter the realm of illusion and impracticability. Moreover, these ideas suffered from the *a priori* contention that a socialist plan has to choose the maximum growth rate. Some more recent attempts to compile forecasts for the long-term outlook in Czechoslovakia do give greater weight to the above dilemma, but, in our view, they have not yet found a satisfactory solution.

Evidence of the fact that we are becoming increasingly conscious of the dilemma is provided by the addition of a new expression − "the coefficient of ignorance" − to our planners' jargon. It is the coefficient by which we have to multiply our forecasting parameters in order to take account of the circumstances that we know about, but are not fully acquainted with. After all, we made a good step forward in our work if we know what is unknown to us and can see the frontiers of our knowledge. We consider that this is a big advance compared with the days when we "knew all the answers", but did not know all the questions.

To determine the parameters of the growth model and formulate a forecast in the framework of a long-term plan, requires a thorough analysis of previous experience. A plan derived from a theoretical analysis of empirical data will, however, be modified again by empirical factors. This implies that the plan that is to provide a firm frame for the operation of newly-released market forces should be regarded rather as a flexible instrument, requiring elaboration in greater detail and adjustment, as soon as further experience is available. It may be expected to assume its final form only when more facts are available about the effect of changes in the operative model and the extent to which it will open up new sources of growth.

## Results of research

The correlation between the system of planning and management, and the strategic parameters of the growth model, has been occupying economists in the socialist countries — and elsewhere — for some years, especially in Poland and Yugoslavia. The problem is not simplified by the fact that some aspects of the developed growth model have not been fully resolved. According to the Polish economist A. Lukaszewicz, some years will probably be needed before the application of the model is quite complete, especially in view of such questions as opening up the model[2] and dealing with amortization, which have not yet been adequately worked out. But the first steps have been taken.

Application of Kalecki's model to empirical data in Poland served in 1959 as the starting point for compiling the first version of Poland's long-term plan for 1961 – 1975.[3] The urgent need for research in the field covered by this chapter was strongly emphasized in 1962 during discussions in Yugo-

---

[2]  I.e., relinquishing the assumption of a closed economy, where foreign trade is not taken into account.

slavia, especially by Prof. Rikard Lange.[4] Interesting, but still inevitably limited results have been published by Prof. Branko Horvat in his work *Towards a Theory of Economic Planning*. The research group Horvat-Sicherl-Nikolić has used a fairly simple multisectoral model to isolate the influence of changes in "the economic system" on the development (decline) of the capital-output ratio in Yugoslavia in the years 1948 – 1964.[5]

In this special and rather difficult field of economic research two distinct, complementary methods of analysis have been employed so far. The fact that Yugoslavia is the only socialist country that has experienced a period of centralized, directive planning and a fairly long period of decentralized, global planning, has led Yugoslav economists to attempt a quantitative investigation into the effectiveness of the two systems, using comparative studies of the growth process and the operation of the main growth factors in the first and second periods. This work, partial results of which have been published and which is still continuing, is, as a rule, based on microeconomic analysis at the sectoral or even enterprise level. A macroeconomic study in comparative economics based on international comparison of four socialist countries has been presented in the two foregoing chapters on the short- and long-term changes in the growth rate. An attempt at further elaboration of the macroeconomic method is the subject of the present chapter.

3  W. LISSOWSKI, *Majetek — Praca — Produkcja*, Warsaw 1962, p. 23.

4  "... three branches of analysis carry special significance: analysis of the influence exerted by the economic system on economic development, analysis of the fundamental laws and tendencies during the rise of and changes in the structure of material production, analysis of the conditions for realizing the products of production." RIKARD LANGE, *Ekonomski Przegląd*, 1961, p. 27.

5  A similar method was used in an article *O dvouletce a první pětiletce* (The Two-Year Plan and the First Five-Year Plan), *Příspěvky k dějinám KSČ*, 1965, no. 3. (The authors J. Flek and J. Goldmann made an attempt to compare the overall effectiveness of the fully centralized management system as it was introduced in 1950 — 52 with the effectiveness of the more or less decentralized system of the earlier transition phase).

## b) Application of the model and its limitations

We have chosen the following procedure for analysing and making an integrated quantification of the correlation between the system of planned management and the leading parameters of the growth model.

### Role of the growth model

First of all, it will be as well to recall what a model actually implies, what purpose it serves and what goals it can achieve. A model is a simplified picture of reality, showing only some of the main quantities and correlations, and abstracting from others. As Prof. Lange has put it[7], a model of the earth's surface can be taken to be a view from a spaceship. As the details recede, the leading features emerge more clearly. Therefore, we should not expect a model of economic growth, especially a fairly simple one, to tell us more than it is able to.

First of all, we need to decide the purpose of our model. It is meant primarily to serve as a demonstration model aimed at the past. We want to illustrate and quantify our theoretical conclusions about the effects of the administrative directive system. In this sense we make no great demands on the model; it serves rather for instruction and illustration. By applying it, we can also demonstrate what could happen if the present intermediate stage were to last too long and develop into a compromise between the old and new management systems.

As for the future, our model is intended as the basis for further work on a specific forecasting model. This, according to Kalecki, should serve as the jumping-off point for the first variant of the long-term plan. Kalecki does not conceive of his model as being purely academic, although its pedagogical value is great. On first reading his book tends to be deceptive, giving the impression of abstractness and a purely theoretical preoccupation. But in reality the genesis of the model was linked with the work on Poland's first long-term plan up to 1975. Its role was, however, confined to the first

---

[7]  O. LANGE, *Politická ekonomie*, Prague, Academia 1966, pp. 103–105, or O. LANGE, *Ekonomia polityczna*, Warsaw 1959, chapter IV.

variant, by which the preliminary growth rate is obtained, the planned rate then being reached by a series of approximations. The point is that with a well-chosen initial base variant, the number of iterations is minimized and the process of plan building shortened. That is the role of Kalecki's model in the methodology of planning; it enables the optimal choice of the initial base variant for plan construction to be made.

Our descriptive model, therefore, has another role. Although building a forecasting model for long-term prognosis involves many other problems, nothing so facilitates this work as experience gained by applying a growth model to empirical data from the past.

One more warning is needed about our attempt toapply Kalecki's model. It concerns the lesson learnt by anyone who has undertaken analytical work with the existing statistical instruments. In choosing an analytical procedure, one has to steer a middle course between the attractive, but dangerous perfectionism that asks more of data and methods than they can give, and ill-considered handling of empirical material.

Furthermore, we have to remember that progress on the thorny path of scientific cognition is bound to be gradual, and it would be foolish to expect to take two steps at once. Nevertheless, our estimate of the net capital-output ratio[8], despite the approximate nature of the assumptions on which it is based, is a certain advance over the usual calculations of grows capital-output ratio.[9]

## Choice of model

The choice of Kalecki's model as the basis of analysis in the present work is in line with the fact that the argument in western growth theory between the post-Keynesians and neo-Classicists had little effect on economic theory in the socialist countries. The model as presented in its fully developed form in Kalecki's *Zarys teorii vzrostu gospodarki socjalistycznej* and in Laski's *Outline of the Theory of Socialist Reproduction* remains for the present the only systematic account of growth theory under socialism. The sole

[8] That is, a ratio freed from the effects of non-investment factors or growth or deceleration.

[9] Not freed from the effects of these factors.

reason is hardly that under Polish conditions — with a manpower surplus — capital was the primary limiting factor, and, consequently, a function of the Harrod-Domar type was indicated. A cogent reason was probably also the existence of strong doubts about the underlying assumptions of the neo-Classist model, even for growth under capitalism. Still more debatable is the question whether, in a planned socialist economy, prices of the factors of production are formed according to the theory of marginal productivity and whether the substitution of factors is governed by the wages-interest link.[10]

One thing is certain — there is no monopoly so dangerous as that in scientific research. Attempts to apply other modern growth models to statistical data of socialist economies are therefore doubly welcome. In the case of Czechoslovakia, an interesting essay has been made by J. Pospíšil to apply the CES function. Some other, on the whole elementary applications, have been made on neo-Classical lines.

In connection with capitalist growth theory, it has been rightly pointed out that "at present it is impossible to give preference to any version (i.e. post-Keynesian or neo-Classicist — our note). Clearly some phenomena can be interpreted more easily using the first version and other with the second."[11] This fact, too, induced the authors to choose the Kalecki model to depict the effects of a highly centralised, directive system of planning and management on the rate of growth.

## Theoretically assumed values for parameters of the demonstration model

In theory, the deepening conflict between the production relations (management system) and productive forces should be manifested in the Kalecki model by substantial changes in the leading parameters of the model — while the $u$-factor, representing the non-investment sources of growth, shrinks, we get a rise — *ceteris paribus* — in the capital-output ratio, and both movements lead to deceleration of growth.

---

[10] G. BOMBACH, „Wirtschaftswachstum", *Handwörterbuch der Sozialwissenschaften*, vol. XII, p. 766.

[11] Ibid., p. 767.

Some difficulty is presented by the question of the degree to which changes observed in the growth rate have been caused a) by the capital-output ratio and investment rate, b) by the $u$-factor. Analyses show that the rate (and hence the capital-output ratio, too) reached a median level around 1957, while the values were higher in the preceding years, partly owing to improved utilization of capacities and manpower reserves, and lower in subsequent years, thanks to the effects of the traditional system of management.

A further complication derives from the nature of the model, which for familiar reasons deals with investment as gross investment, just as it uses gross data for the national income. The parameter $a$ is therefore introduced into the model as a corrective. Its role consists in accounting for the influence on the growth rate of the gross national income of physical writing-off of capital assets. In the first years of the period of investigation, this "amortization" coefficient was evidently quite low (in absolute terms) but in the course of time its significance was somewhat increased. Consequently, the difference $(u - a)$, representing the combined effect of a) non-investment growth sources and b) physical write-off of capital assets, may affect the growth more strongly than the parameter $u$ by itself.

Increase in the capital-output ratio needs to be broken down to a) effect of structural changes, b) operation of the traditional model, c) the (residual) effect of the given type and rate of technological advance.

Disaggregation of Kalecki's $u$-parameter is also fraught with difficulty, because non-investment growth sources are hard to locate and still more hard to quantify. The main components, as far as Czechoslovakia is concerned, are evidently: relatively unfavourable trend of the input – output relation (especially in recent years) stemming from the negative effects produced by the traditional model of planning and management; gradual exhaustion of the capacity and manpower reserves that were released by socializing the means of production and introducing economic planning; changes in the growth rates of inventories and capital-under-construction in relation to the growth rate of the economy. The consequences of alienation and growing bureaucracy within a hierarchically structured economy are evidently as difficult to isolate and quantify within the $u$-factor as it is to determine the influence of technological advance on the capital-output ratio.

## c) Procedure chosen for statistical estimation of parameters of the growth model

In contrast to the above theoretical considerations, to fill in the model statistically calls for some important simplifications – at least in the first approximation. In order to carry out disaggregation of changes observed in the growth rate, on the one hand to the $u$-factor effect and, on the other, to the effect of the capital-output ratio and investment rate, we will assume that the capital-output ratio is constant at its average level over the entire period. This hypothesis of stability can perhaps be justified as the product of two opposed tendencies – on the one hand, a rising trend for the factor evoked by operation of the traditional management system (e.g. rising investment costs per unit capacity in building a cement works), on the other, a falling trend in line with the type of technological progress prevailing over the last thirty years in advanced capitalist countries. (E.g. sinking investment costs per unit capacity in building thermo-power stations).

This implies, of course, that compensation of an otherwise possible drop in the capital-output ratio by the negative effects of the traditional system on the growth rate has to be seen as a phenomenon carrying similar consequences to those of the other leakages already examined above. (A rising capital-output ratio means that capital equipment advances more rapidly than productivity of labour). The directive management system started this trend, because it regarded capital assets as free goods.[12]

The more detailed analysis of the capital-output ratio into three components, as suggested above, will therefore have to wait for further research. In view of the comparatively small extent of structural changes in investment construction since 1950, this procedure seems permissible for the first approximation. This is confirmed by information from the Czechoslovak Institute of Economic Planning on the slight influence exerted by structural changes on the capital-output ratio.

Disaggregation of the $u$-factor will be carried out as follows: we shall distinguish between its positive component $u_1$, representing the results of technological and organizational improvement, and its negative component

---

[12] Cf. K. K. KURIHARA, *National Income and Economic Growth*, London 1961, pp. 134–5.

induced by the traditional system. We shall assume that this latter component is composed of a negative, linear deceleration element $(u_2)$, the decelerating (or accelerating) effect of excessive accumulation (or disaccumulation) in circulating assets, i.e. inventories and capital-under-construction $(u_3)$ and, finally, the influence of quasi-cyclical and chance fluctuations $(u_4)$.

From these considerations it follows that in place of Kalecki's basis formula

$$r = \frac{1}{m}\frac{I}{D} + u - a \tag{1}$$

where $r$ = observed growth rate of national income (gross)
  $m$ = net (incremental) capital-output ratio
  $I$ = volume of productive capacities put into operation in the current year
  $D$ = national income gross (i.e. gross of write-offs)
  $u$ = non-investment growth factors
  $a$ = amortization factor

we shall employ the adjusted growth model

$$r = \frac{1}{m}\frac{I}{D} + (u_1 + u_2 - a) + (u_3 + u_4) \tag{2}$$

## Correlation analysis

Multiple correlation analysis (with investment rate and time as independent variables and growth rate as a dependent variable) gives us both the value of the capital-output ratio $m$, and the value of the sum $(u_1 + u_2 - a)$, as well as the value of the theoretical (computed) growth rate $r'$. We then have

$$r' = \frac{1}{m}\frac{I}{D} + (u_1 + u_2 - a/t + c) \tag{3}$$

where $r'$ = growth rate computed from model
  $t$ = distance (in years) from start of chronological series
  $c$ = constant

$$r - r' = (u_3 + u_4).$$

From the correlation analysis we then have the solution of equation (3):

$$r' = 0.48 \frac{I}{D} - 0.81t + 5.04 \qquad (4)$$

The results of the analysis are seen in diagram 3. The coefficient of multiple correlation, adjusted for size of selection and number of degrees of freedom, is $R = 0.69$. This coefficient is relatively high. It has to be taken into account that the variables not explained by the chosen regression equation include deviations from the computed values for the growth rate $u_3$ (excessive accumulation – or disaccumulation – in circulating assets) and $u_4$ (where quasi-cyclical, not chance fluctuation is concerned), which are part of the system of functional dependence under investigation, although they are not explicitly included in the regression analysis.

We give below a more detailed description of the method by which the values of individual quantities were obtained.

## Non-investment growth factor $u_1$ (Kalecki's u-factor)

The first of the four components of Kalecki's non-investment growth factor $u$, termed $u_1$, represents the $u$-factor in the precise sense according to his model. That is to say, it expresses growth in gross national income flowing from factors other than investment. It thus covers increment in the national income deriving from technological and organizational measures that – at least in principle – do not call for supplementary investment inputs. It is, therefore, allied to the coefficient that is elsewhere termed the coefficient of utilization. Its value (amounting to 1.3) was estimated from numerous published technico-economic indicators expressing the degree of intensive or extensive utilization of basic types of machinery and equipment in various industrial and transportation sectors.[13]

---

[13] When we follow the course of the time series $u_1$, we are of course dealing with cyclical development. However, these changes do not reflect changes in the effectiveness of technological and organizational measures, but changes in the effectiveness of the whole system that is alternating between acceleration and deceleration. Therefore we have confined ourselves, as far as $u_1$ is concerned, to a long-term linear trend.

In estimating $u_1$, we had to bear in mind that the weighted average of technico-economic indicators of utilization of production capacities gives an unduly ascending trend to the $u_1$ factor. There are two reasons: firstly, the technico-economic indicators that are consistently followed in the traditional system are usually more favourable than those that are not statistically recorded, simply because they are often "slogged" at the expense of others; secondly, improvement in the indicators of production-capacity utilization does not stem solely from technical and organizational measures in Kalecki's sense, that is from non-investment growth sources. Improvement is also caused by gradual rejuvenation of the production apparatus, because newly-built capacities are usually better designed. The upward distortion of factor $u_1$ has been compensated in our estimate — completely or at least partially — by the fact that most of the data available to us started from 1954. This eliminated earlier development when this factor was probably substantially higher.

Another factor component, $u_2$, is intended to record the deceleration effect exerted on the growth rate by the traditional management system under changing conditions. This component was obtained as described below.

*The amortization factor.* Determination of the *a*-factor (representing the annual reduction in gross national income due to physical write-off of obsolete capital assets in production is somewhat easier. Statistical data give us the write-off of capital assets in proportion to their total volume. The question of how effective these assets were before being written off is rather more difficult. However, any error in estimating effectiveness plays no great part in constructing the demonstration model.

The available data show that between 0·8 per cent (in 1950) and 1·3 per cent (1964) of the total volume of capital assets (valued at full replacement value) was written off annually. The average effectiveness of these assets can be taken to be roughly equal to the average for all capital assets in production, because it can be assumed that before being dropped from the production process they were kept in reasonable condition by general maintenance and repair. So we have $a = -0·8$ for 1950 and $-1·3$ for 1964.

To facilitate the analysis we will work at the given stage, however, with the average value $a = 1·0$. (The traditional system affects the *a*-factor by keeping it — despite some growth — permanently below its optimal level). In the short term this accelerates growth, but this is a Pyrrhic victory in the long run. The long-term outcome is, in fact, a drop in the potential growth rate owing to the resultant deterioration in the capital-output ratio).[14]

**No. 7. Growth rate of the national income by factors of growth or deceleration**

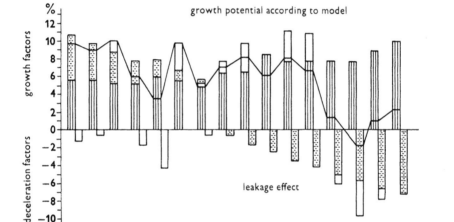

factors of growth — deceleration

▤ investment (capacity increments)

▦ non-investment (linear) ($u_1 + u_2 - a$)

▢ excessive accumulation in circulating assets ($u_3$); wave-like and chance fluctuation ($u_4$)

── observed growth rate

*Non-investment growth factor $u_2$, expressing the negative, decelerating effect to the traditional management system on the growth rate.* The values for the overall effect on the growth rate of linearly operating non-investment factors of growth (or deceleration) — i.e. factors expressed by ($u_1 + u_2 =$

---

[14] With further approximation to reality — that is, if we drop the assumption of a stable $a$-factor — an interesting problem arises. If the factor sinks from $-0.8$ to $-1.3$, then (with a linear trend confirmed by a point diagram) $u_1$ or $u_2$ must have increased.

$= a)$ — were obtained, as mentioned above, by multiple correlation analysis. Having thus obtained a value for the expression $(u_1 + u_2 - a)$ of $-0.81$, and knowing the value of $u_1$, and of $a$ from earlier estimates, we could get the residual value for $u_2$ from the equation

$$1.3 + u_2 - 1.0 = -0.8$$

Since the value $u_2$ was obtained residually, its estimate naturally lies within a fairly wide range of possible error. But it is a demonstration model that makes no claims to precision in numerical results.

*Capital-output ratio m.* By multiple correlation analysis we have obtained a value for the sum of three parameters in Kalecki's growth model (factors $a$, $u_1$, $u_2$), and the value of the capital-output ratio $m$.

**No. 8. Dependence of the growth rate freed of the effect of non-investment sources of growth or deceleration on the investment rate**

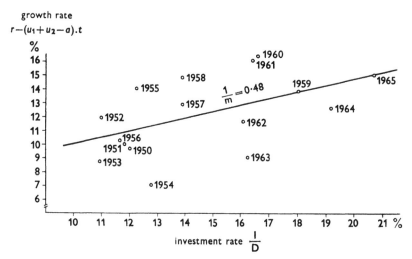

The relevant results of correlation analysis are depicted on a point diagram (Diagram 8). It shows that the growth rate, freed of non-investment sources of growth or deceleration (i.e. reduced by the value of $(u_1 + u_2 - a)$, has an upward trend of about 0·5 per cent for every one per cent increment in the investment rate $(I/D)$. (When $\alpha$ is the angle contained by the regression line $1/m$ and the horizontal axis $I/D$, then tg $\alpha$ equals 0·48, which is equal to the reciprocal value of the capital-output ratio $m = 2\cdot08$).

For the above correlation analysis, the values of the investment rate $I/D$ were taken from published data on national income (raised by write-offs) and on capital assets flowing from construction.

In view of the relatively small annual variation in the flow of new production capacities, account was not taken of possible time lags between putting into operation and starting up full-scale production. Nevertheless, the circular (or more precisely, spiral) sequence observed for $1950-6$ and $1959-65$ (anticlockwise) indicates that changes in the growth rate exhibit a time lag behind changes in the investment rate, as was to be expected.[15] This fairly inconsiderable time lag has been ignored in the first approximation.

In the light of this correlation analysis it was possible to divide the growth rate observed into a component stemming from investment sources and a component gained from non-investment sources of growth. (For calculation, see Table 10).

*Other non-investment sources of growth or deceleration, $u_3$ $u_4$.* Correlation analysis further provided deviations between the theoretical growth rate values, determined by our illustrative model, and those observed. These deviations are expressed by component $u_3$ and by $u_4$.

We then have

$$r - r' = r - \left[\frac{1}{m}\frac{I}{D} + (u_1 + u_2 - a)\,t + c\right] = (u_3 + u_4)\,. \qquad (5)$$

Component $u_3$ expresses the deceleration effect exerted on the national income by excessive investment in circulating assets, i.e. in inventories and capital-under-construction; alternatively, it expresses the acceleration effect of relative disinvestment on the growth rate of the national income. Component $u_4$, then, as already stated, covers the effect of quasi-cyclical and chance fluctuations on the growth rate.

[15] Cf. M. KALECKI, *Economic Dynamics*, London 1954, pp. 106−110.

108

However, theoretical considerations and practical calculations demonstrate that excessive inventory growth is more likely to depress the growth of final consumption, rather than to retard the growth of national income by means of cutting investments in operative capital assets.

Consequently, it has become impossible — at least for the time being — to separate components $u_3$ and $u_4$ as far as their decelerating or accelerating effect on the growth rate is concerned. What is more, there are reasons for believing that separation is not even necessary, because component $u_3$ also represents a phenomenal form, indeed a special mechanism of wave-like movement in the growth rate, although with a marked time lag.

Quite "reasonable" behaviour by the time series of residual value $(u_3 + u_4)$ — more precisely, its behaviour according to theoretical expectation (see *Diagram No. 6*) — gives some certainty as to the reliability of the model with regard to the methods used in constructing the illustrative model and the validity of the results it yields. Moreover, the value obtained for the incremental capital-output ratio, $m = 2 \cdot 08$, which is in general agreement with other empirical results, confirms these conclusions. Similarly, it is possible to evaluate occurrences of theoretically expected circular movements in *Diagram No. 7*.

## Indirect and direct analysis of the growth process

In our account so far we have relied exclusively on indirect analysis of the growth process, i.e. on analysis according to the development of capital assets and their effectiveness. Especially in view of the analytical methods customary in Czechoslovakia, it would be necessary to supplement indirect analysis by direct, using the formula

$$r = \frac{1}{m} \frac{I}{D} + u - a = \alpha + \beta$$

where $\alpha$ is the growth rate of labour productivity,

$\beta$ is the growth rate of employment in the production sphere.

By examining the effect of changes in employment on the parameters of the growth model, we would evidently arrive at interesting results.

## d) Overall results of analysis

For a better presentation of the main results yielded by our work we have included Diagram 6, in which the beneficial effect of the administrative-directive system of planning and management during the first years of the period under investigation[16], and its negative influence in recent years, emerge with great clarity. The values for the growth rates observed are analysed in this diagram from the standpoint of the effects brought about by changes in the investment rate and with regard to the influence of non-investment sources of growth or deceleration. These, in their turn, are broken down to the net effect of changes in the expression $(u_1 + u_2 = a)$ i.e. com-

**Table 10.** *Growth rate of the national income (gross) computed from the model*
$$r = 1m \cdot I/D + (u_1 + u_2 - a/t = r' = 1/2.08 \cdot I/D - 0 \cdot 81t + 5 \cdot 04$$

| Year | $r$ | $I/D$ | $t$ | $1/m \cdot I/D =$ $= 0 \cdot 48(I/D)$ | $(u_1 + u_2 -$ $- a)t =$ $= -0 \cdot 81t$ | $c = 5 \cdot 04$ | $r' = (5) +$ $+ (6) + (7)$ |
|---|---|---|---|---|---|---|---|
| (1) | (2) | (3) | (4) | (5) | (6) | (7) | (8) |
| 1950 | 9·7 | 12·0 | 0 | 5·76 | 0·00 | 5·04 | 10·80 |
| 1951 | 9·2 | 11·8 | 1 | 5·66 | − 0·81 | 5·04 | 9·89 |
| 1952 | 10·3 | 11·0 | 2 | 5·28 | − 1·62 | 5·04 | 8·70 |
| 1953 | 6·3 | 10·9 | 3 | 5·23 | − 2·43 | 5·04 | 7·84 |
| 1954 | 3·7 | 12·8 | 4 | 6·14 | − 3·24 | 5·04 | 7·94 |
| 1955 | 10·0 | 12·3 | 5 | 5·90 | − 4·05 | 5·04 | 6·89 |
| 1956 | 5·3 | 11·7 | 6 | 5·62 | − 4·86 | 5·04 | 5·80 |
| 1957 | 7·2 | 13·9 | 7 | 6·67 | − 5·67 | 5·04 | 6·04 |
| 1958 | 8·3 | 13·9 | 8 | 6·67 | − 6·48 | 5·04 | 5·23 |
| 1959 | 6·4 | 18·0 | 9 | 8·64 | − 7·29 | 5·04 | 6·39 |
| 1960 | 8·2 | 16·7 | 10 | 8·02 | − 8·10 | 5·04 | 4·96 |
| 1961 | 7·0 | 16·5 | 11 | 7·92 | − 8·91 | 5·04 | 4·05 |
| 1962 | 1·8 | 16·1 | 12 | 7·73 | − 9·72 | 5·04 | 3·05 |
| 1963 | −1·6 | 16·3 | 13 | 7·82 | −10·53 | 5·04 | 2·33 |
| 1964 | 1·2 | 19·1 | 14 | 9·17 | −11·34 | 5·04 | 2·87 |
| 1965 | 2·8 | 20·7 | 15 | 9·94 | −12·15 | 5·04 | 2·83 |

[16] Primarily, however, there was the effect of accelerative changes in production relations irrespective of the model of planning and management.

binations of the $u$-factor; further, to the negative (or sometimes positive) effect stemming from excessive investment in (or disinvestment from) circulating assets, $(u_3)$ and the residual effect $(u_4)$ of quasi-cyclical and chance fluctuations in the growth rate. (For numerical values see Table 10).

## Role of investment

The diagram reveals especially clearly the changing role played in growth by investments. While in the first years they tended to be in the background, in the second half of the fifties they emerged as the leading growth factor. But in the sixties their beneficial effect is already offset by deceleration factors.

It is precisely the limited scope for non-investment growth factors (including the growing burden of maintenance, and costs of repair and renewal) that stands in the way of transition from the initial to a higher stage of socialist construction. In the terms of the analysis by the growth model, it constrains the transition from a growth strategy based on reserves of labour and capacities to a type of growth strategy corresponding to conditions of full employment and aimed at full utilization of capital production assets. Simultaneously, this transition requires a corresponding radical change in the model of economic operation.

Given the state of our knowledge today, this conclusion might seem to be a statement of the obvious. Indeed the majority of economists in Czechoslovakia and a substantial number of economists elsewhere (according to the specific situation in each socialist country) would probably put their names to the above statement without hesitation. But not all. And, as far as Czechoslovakia is concerned, prompt implementation of the new system calls for some big changes in the habits of thought among all concerned with economics, in practice and theory.

## Growth potential of the Czechoslovak economy

Another point that emerges clearly from Diagram 6 is the great growth potential shown by the Czechoslovak economy in recent years. The magnitude of this potential can be estimated as follows: as mentioned above, the investment effect of 1961 – 5 was offset (either partially or completely) by leakages. The investments concerned have, therefore, not yet yielded their appropriate result in economic growth. Expressed in the potential effect on the growth rate of the national income, the volume of investment expenditure in 1962 – 5 could yield a growth of 36 per cent (i.e. the sum of amounts in column 5, Table 10). The actual overall growth was, however, only 4 per cent (i.e. the sum of amounts in column 2, Table 10). Consequently, it would be possible to ensure by degrees an increase in national income of about one-fifth, with almost no addition of production capacity. This growth potential can, in fact, be harnessed by degrees if the provision of all the essential conditions for an accelerated and at the same time thorough introduction of the new system manages to transform the present leakages into supplementary sources of growth.

In reality, the growth potential of the Czechoslovak economy in relation to the present national income is considerably higher than indicated by the above estimate, which is intended merely as a first approximation. We should bear in mind that the leakages existing hitherto have a cumulative effect, which grows according to the familiar formula of compound interest, while our estimate is restricted to the 1961 – 5 period.

With the present state of our knowledge, it is clearly impossible to make a direct assessment of another component in the growth potential, which is perhaps still more significant than the one cited. This component relates to supplementary growth sources which could be brought into action by thorough implementation of the new system. It could remove, or at least cut back, the leakages that cannot, at present, be quantified, such as alienation and growth of bureaucratic elements in a hierarchically organized system of directive and administrative planning and management.

## Technical advantages of the method of analysis chosen

From the technical angle the advantage of the method of analysis chosen here is that the greater part of the $u$-factor i.e. components $u_1$, $u_2$ and $u_3$ can be obtained from statistical data[17] and only a smaller part residu-

[17] The value $u_2$ was, in fact, also obtained residually, but from the results of the analysis in Chapter V possibilities exist for its independent estimaton.

ally. As Prof. Laski has rightly stressed,[18] determination of the $u$-factor (and its components) calls for some simplifying assumptions. Although there is simplification, this is an essential step towards an understanding of economic reality.

In contrast, the Cobb-Douglas type of computation involves up to 50 per cent of observed variations being ascribed to a residual factor. This is variously interpreted (without further disaggregation) either as technological advance or investment in the human factor etc.

## Forecasting and decision model

In the light of the above conclusions, we consider that the present work has adequately demonstrated that the empirically applied growth model is suitable for the purpose we have suggested, that is, as a criterion of the effectiveness of the given system of planning and management, despite all the limitations and simplifications that are unavoidable in a first approximation. Moreover, opportunities offer for employing the model for other purposes, too.

Although many fresh problems arise in constructing a forecasting model for long-term prognosis, experience with applying growth models to empirical data from the past can facilitate the work. And such experience in applying the Kalecki's model points to its suitability — after necessary elaboration and further discussion — for the first stage of forecasting long-term economic development, as has, in fact, been demonstrated in Poland.

Our model could also serve as a decision model. If — theoretically — the decision had to be taken again whether to keep the old management system or introduce a new one, the question could be put to the model what would be the most probable growth assuming the old system continued to operate — say to the end of the sixties. By mounting the relevant values into our model ($t = 20$, $I/D = 15\%$, i.e. approximately the average value for $I/D$ to date), we get r = −4 per cent. Adding the probable effect of components $u_3$ and $u_4$, which was both in 1954 and 1963 approximately −4 per

[18] K. LASKI, *The Factors of Growth of National Income in a Socialist Economy*, Studies on the Theory of Reproduction and Prices, Warsaw 1964, p. 165.

cent, we get a statistical estimate for the "growth" rate in 1970 of −8 per cent. This is a warning signal, which should be noted while there is yet time by those who still recommend various alternatives to thorough and speedy implementation of the new system of planning and management.

### *"Growth potential" of Czechoslovak economic theory*

The model would appear to be relevant to the growth potential of economic theory in Czechoslovakia, too. As we have tried to demonstrate, analysis of past economic development by applying Kalecki's model of growth under socialism shows that the Czechoslovak economy possesses a growth potential that is probably among the largest of all socialist countries. Such a finding can play quite an important part at a time when both over-optimism, and excessive pessimism, both of which are to be found among economists today, are potentially dangerous and could harm the economy. It would be equally wrong to give undue weight to the revival of the past two years and overestimate its probable duration, as it would be dangerous to give any absolute value to the recently discovered barriers to growth. A common search for economically justified paths between the pitfalls of excessive optimism and pessimism could contribute to enabling economic theory to become a productive force in its own right to a greater extent than has been the case in recent years.

Chapter VII

# The Principle of Rational Operation and Economic Growth

"We occupy a special place among the countries that have taken the path of economic planning, and therefore our opportunities are especially big, too. Other countries, such as the Soviet Union, Poland, Yugoslavia, Rumania, either now, or like the Soviet Union, thirty years ago, took the new road with a production apparatus and experience taken over not from the capitalist age, but in large measure from the precapitalist era. We are the first country to take this road with an enormous staff of commercial men, experts, people with a wealth of experience. If we prove capable of getting it all together and adding modern, efficient administrative methods, we shall be able to go further in a short time than other countries with planned economies. If we fail to realize that this is among the key elements in our prospects, it will not be too bad, but in any case we shall lose time."

LUDVÍK FREJKA, 1948

The shortcomings of the administrative, directive system of planning and management in the circumstances that have evolved over the past decade are most fully expressed in the substantial loss of effectiveness shown by economic calculation; this, too, is the main reason why the system has been transformed from a growth factor into a barrier to growth. The outcome is to undermine the supreme principle, that of rational operation. Economic calculation is a set of evaluations that are essential if the economic agent is to conduct economic decision-making, i.e. choose the most rational method of attaining the goal of his activity. The endeavour to achieve the maximum result with given inputs (in other words, to achieve minimum inputs for a given result) expresses the principle of rational operation. Economic calculation is the method of implementing this principle.

115

## a)   In retrospect

In the days of the personality cult, under the influence of centralized planned management, economic theory, which was often a mere reflection or simply a description of existing practical measures, came to be dominated by the view that the only conceivable method of managing a socialist economy was to concentrate initiave and decision-making at the centre.

To grasp the theoretical significance of economic calculation, especially for a socialist economy, we need to take a brief look at the history of this category. The principle of rational operation emerged as the groundwork of economic activity only in the early days of capitalism. Essentially it implies comparing inputs (means) and earnings (ends). Rational decision-making is that in which the ratio of inputs and output is most favourable. Every capitalist concern aims at maximum profit − profit is the goal of its activity. The actitivity of self-sufficient producers, typified by a multiplicity of aims and by traditional methods of production handed down from generation to generation, was replaced, with the advent of capitalism and the full victory of commodity production, by activity for profit. All partial operations were then united in the single aim of profit, and to this end there was a continual endeavour to improve methods of production. In aspiring to the highest profit, a capitalist enterprise therefore adopts the principle of economizing: the lower the money costs and the higher the earnings, the greater the profit. The principle of economical working is reflected in a capitalist enterprise in an essentially effective organization of the production process.

But the principle of rationality is limited in a capitalist economy to enterprises. In the macroeconomic field − that of the entire economy − conditions are lacking for its consistent application. The obstacle is the private ownership of the means of production. That is why so many elements of irrationality are evinced in a capitalist economy taken as a whole − the most typical being unemployment, depression and crisis.

Only with the advent of socialism does the principle of rational operation and economic calculation find conditions for its full implementation. In the macroeconomic field this derives from the socialist relations of production − from planned management of the economy. Socialist production relations imply that the immediate goal of economic activity is to satisfy the wants of the population. In a socialist economy economic calculation

116

(*rachunek ekonomiczny, Wirtschaftliche Rechnungsführung*) thereby acquires new meaning. The rationality of enterprise operation conducted by private capital is complemented by rationality throughout the economy. The goal is changed, because the aim of the enterprises singly (maximum profit) is subordinated to a higher society-wide aim (steady rise of personal and social consumption, steadily improving conditions for the development of the human personality). The expression of this higher social aim is the economic plan. And that is why it is necessary to ensure full application of economic calculation at all levels of management throughout the reproduction process. The goals of single enterprises are no longer isolated and autonomous, because after socialization of the means of production, the entire economy is managed by a single system of planning and management for society as a whole. The fact that economic calculation can now be employed throughout the economy provides the opportunity to implement rational operation to the full on a wider scale than that of single enterprises. Indeed, this is one of the advantages of the socialist over the capitalist system.

This implies that the principle of rational operation cannot be considered apart from the relations of production; the area within which it operates and its character are conditioned by the type of production relations in force. What is more, a strong element characterizing given production relations is the possibility and mode of use, and the area of operation of this principle (economic rationality).

Nevertheless, the opportunity to place the entire economy on a strict basis of economic calculation, and the opportunity to attain thereby a state of rational operation throughout the socialist economy, has not yet been fully realized in practice. The degree to which the opportunities are used depends in large measure on the level achieved in methods of economic planning and management.[1]

---

[1] A hierarchical structure of goals is a special expression of planning the social economy, an expression of integration of the aims of socialist enterprises with the main goal stated in the plan of socialist economy. It is an expression of socio-economic rationality in the socialist mode of production. This rationality expressed by the hierarchical arrangement of goals does not come ready-made as soon as socialist economic conditions are established. It evolves gradually, with difficulty and alongside the growth of the socialist mode of production. (O. LANGE, *Ekonomia polityczna*, Warsaw 1959, pp. 158—159.

The most favourable conditions for applying the principle of economic calculation at the enterprise and national level are offered by a system of socialist management in which the society-wide plan is linked with the market mechanism.

The fruitful idea of linking the plan to operation of the law of value and the market mechanism belonged to the *avant-garde* thinking and theoretical armoury of Marxist economic theory as early as the twenties. The genesis of this central theme running through discussions among several generations of Marxist economists is highly instructive and still awaits thorough evaluation.

The abnormal economic conditions obtaining during the period of war communism helped to reinforce the pre-revolutionary idea of socialism as a self-sufficient and centrally directed economy.[2] The first breach made in this traditional view during the twenties appears − in confrontation with the subsequently prevailing attitude to the plan and the market current during the Stalin era of economic thinking − as a far-reaching revolutionary act. Nevertheless, it still bears traces of earlier ideas about the possibility of overcoming the market under normal conditions of socialist economic development.[3]

[2] N. Bukharin was for a time among the outstanding representatives of the concept of economic processes based on natural relations of production during the transition to socialism. In a book published in 1922 he expressed pre-revolutionary views on the socialist economy, as for example the following: "... the natural-material consideration assumes decisive importance, and hence distribution of social production into various spheres of 'concrete' labour also acquires exceptional importance." N. BUKHARIN, *Oekonomie der Transformationsperiode*, Verlag der KI, 1922, p. 199.

[3] "In the sphere of distribution the task of Soviet power is now to continue unswervingly to replace trade by planned distribution of products, organised on a nation-wide scale ... It is impossible to abolish money in the first period of transition from capitalism to communism ... The CPR will endeavour to carry out with maximum speed the most radical measures in preparation for abolishing money, primarily replacing it by savings books, cheques, short-term vouchers for receipt of social products etc., introduction of an obligation to deposit money in banks and so on. Practical experience in preparing and carrying out such measures will show which are the most effective." See V. I. LENIN, Draft Programme of the CPR(b), February−March 1919 − *Works*, vol. 29 (Czech edition) pp. 129−130. "The CPR, which has to direct the renewal of the economy in the Soviet Republic,

One can follow how, at a later stage, the discussion on the plan, the law of value and the market developed into a general consideration of the mechanism by which a socialist economy operates and of the best methods of management. The ideas about the plan and the market, linking the regulatory activity of the market with effective administrative measures, and about the necessity for enterprises to have freedom on the market and so on appear highly topical today.[4] A fuller evaluation of war communism led to the

---

will have, in pursuing this policy further, to devote the most careful attention to the economic situation, the most typical features of which should be seen as: 1. creation of an internal market as a result of abolishing compulsory handing over of all surpluses and 2. development of monetary circulation. Both are immediate consequences of the petit-bourgeois type of economy prevailing in the country ... In this situation, the main task of the CPR in the economic field is to see that Soviet power guides economic activity in such a way that it will base its policy on the existence of the market and take account of its laws, that it will control the market and, by means of systematic, precisely-considered economic measures based on exact information about the market process, will take the management of the market and money circulation into its own hands." (Eleventh All-Russian Conference of the CPR(b), December 1921, translated from *KSSS v rezolucích a usneseních sjezdů, konferencí a plenárních zasedání ÚV, part I*, Prague 1954, p. 508).

[4]  "All preceding experiences have, however, shown that a plan of a socialist economy cannot be stated *a priori* by theoretical or bureaucratic means. A genuine socialist economic plan, covering all industrial sectors in their interrelationships, and the interrelationship between industry in its entirety and agriculture, is possible solely as the result of long-term economic experience based on nationalisation and a lasting endeavour to achieve practical coordination of various economic sectors and correct records of results.

For the immediate period this job is, therefore, one of general regulation and, in large measure, of preparation. It cannot simply be laid down by some formula, but assumes that in its main tasks, its methods and practice, the controlling economic apparatus will constantly and carefully adapt its targets and conditions to the market. Only in their final stage will planning methods be able, and have to, take control of the market and thereby abolish it.

From the above there quite obviously arise two dangers connected with applying methods of state economic planning in the coming phase: a) when attempting to outstrip economic development by means of planned interventions, to replace the regulatory activity of the market by administrative measures for which the ground has not been prepared by actual economic experience, partial or general economic crises of the specific type observed in the period of war communism ("choking up",

realization that whenever, in view of exceptional circumstances, the principle of economic rationality is infringed, there are losses in the economy and the costs of revolution are raised. The experience of economic management in the days of NEP confirmed that the plan-market link was the factor making it possible to implement *khozraschot*, that is economic calculation as an instrument making for rational operation, based on the endeavour (stated in general terms) to achieve maximum performance with minimum outlay.

Nevertheless, it seems that in a sense the course of research and management methods went into reverse in the latter half of the twenties. How else to explain the dominance of rigid centralism, which came into conflict with law of value employed in the main purely as a means of recording? The switch in theoretical views on the plan and the market that took place in the late twenties and early thirties was primarily induced by the need for rapid industrial growth in the first socialist country and the necessity of mobilizing and redistributing the sources of accumulation, both non-socialist and publicly-owned, at the centre. The first land of socialism paid dearly for its precipitate industrialization of a backward economy with inadequate resources for internal socialist accumulation. Growth in consumption as a limiting factor of accumulation and the principle of economic rationality came into conflict with the rate and type of economic growth. In face of this situation, the choice fell to the method of rigid central management of the reproduction process, with the emphasis in planning on administrative forms, in short the ideas and instruments typical for a directive model of planned management.

---

"closure" etc.) are inevitable; b) should central regulation lag behind patently urgent needs, economic issues will come to be resolved by uneconomical market methods even in cases where prompt administrative intervention could achieve the same results in a shorter time and with smaller loss of effort and means.

Since we have gone over to market forms of economy, the State must allow individual enterprises the essential freedom for economic activities on the market and may not try to substitute administrative decision. If, however, every trust whose work is to be successful should feel that its hands are free, and if it is to bear full responsibility for its work, on the other hand the State should see trusts and other associations as bodies serving it, by the help of which it explores the market, and this enables it to take a number of practical measures that run ahead of the alignment adopted by individual enterprises or associations on the market." (Twelfth Congress of the CPR(b), 17—25 April, 1923, *KSSS* ibid., pp. 595—6.)

More or less implicit in this model of economic operation is a contradiction between the level and methods of central management, with its predominantly administrative instruments, on the one hand, and the law of value plus the principle of rational operation, on the other. The principles of the model can be the basis for different practical systems of management. The directive model can be regarded as a lower type of planned management because it reduces the scope for implementing the principle of rationality. It is appropriate to abnormal conditions of economic development and is conditioned by technological and economic backwardness, need for rapid structural shifts, or a war economy and defence priorities.

In the phase of Stalinist economic thinking — with its inherent empiricism, lack of subtle methods in theoretical analysis, insistence on the absolute validity of superficial phenomena in economic life and historically conditioned forms — the directive model of economic operation was held to be an organic part of a socialist economy, indeed the sole possible method of planned management. Value instruments and the market mechanism appeared as alien elements that interfered with planned development. For a time the prevailing view was that the law of value and commodity-money relations had to be progressively curbed, which led in practice to degeneration of economic calculation.

## b) Degeneration of economic calculation in the administrative directive system of management

Despite the big opportunities offered by the socialist order for full development of the productive forces, for a time the course was retrogressive in the sphere of implementing the principles of rational operation. As the administrative management system gained ground, there was inevitably a corresponding decline, even degeneration, in the application of economic calculation.

With the change-over to a fully centralized, administrative system of planning and management, the goals placed before production enterprises were radically altered; pride of place was occupied by the volume of output, while the costs incurred took second place. Fulfilling and overfulfilling production targets overshadowed any consideration of rational operation as commonly understood. The requirement that an enterprise should consistently weigh up inputs and outputs and so maximize profit therefore receded into the background. The decisive yardstick of performance was comparison of output with the targets set in the production plan.

The responsibility for safeguarding the principles of rational operation was taken over by the superior authority that laid down the production plan and the plan of operating costs. But with the limited information at its disposal and the conflict between its interests and those of enterprises, the job of ensuring minimal costs in subordinated enterprises was extremely difficult, if not impossible, for such an authority.

When the market mechanism had been eliminated, production costs, earnings, profit and prices ceased to be criteria for enterprise decision-making and for assessing performance. Financial operations in an enterprise turned into a passive reflection of the reproduction process, which was untouched by market signals because it was almost exclusively directed by administration — from the top, at that — depriving enterprises of all opportunities to choose their goals and the means whereby they might maximize profit or minimize costs. Value categories inevitably degenerated into mere instruments of recording and control. Economic calculation, which had hitherto served as a highly effective instrument of rational operation (at least in the microeconomic sphere), was transformed into a formal version of *khozraschot*, almost completely divorced from economic processes. The very concept of "economic calculation" fell into oblivion.

The principle of *khozraschot* was first postulated in government documents of the twenties[5], and in professional journals: "What does the *khozraschot* principle mean? It means management of the economy with a view to attaining the maximum result with the minimum outlay... In the language of economic theory, it means to revive the operation of the law of value with various restrictions stemming from the specific features of the Soviet economy."

We have here a clear and brief definition. But most interesting of all, there is mention of the intimate connection of khozrashchot, rationality on a society-wide scale and the specific operation of the law of value under socialism. If the statement were not forty years old, it would seem like

---

[5]    Decree of the All-Union *Sovnarkhoz*, July 11, 1921.

a highly topical contribution to our recent discussions on planned management of the national economy. And as if the author sensed the objections with which his views would be met even in the years to come, he continued:

"This contention meets with opposition among many economists. They usually justify their opposition by saying that law of value is a product of capitalism, and we, after all, are building socialism. Further objections concern the fact that the law of value is the regulator of the anarchy in the capitalist mode of production and is unsuited to a planned economy. Excessive abstraction and a cut-and-dried approach prevent these economists from grasping the heart of the matter. The fact is that, at the present time, we are experiencing a stage in the building up of socialism when many of the economic categories of capitalism are still operative. The law of value can be compared to a machine-gun, which serves him who aims it. The attempt to see the law of value and the plan as mutually exclusive elements means nothing else than to return anew to the problem of the plan-market relation under NEP, which life has already resolved."[6]

The institution of *khozraschot* in the NEP period considerably extended the role of commodity-money relations compared with the days of war communism, and in a sense gave them greater importance. In the *khozraschot* system of planned allocation (distribution) of production factors, exchange does not take place without money. The movements of material assets are matched by movements of money. This, to some extent, justifies the formulation that in the *khozraschot* system distribution of the amount of living and past labour at the disposal of society is carried out in a commodity-money form. However, money is not in the centralized directive model an active instrument for influencing the movements of material factors in reproduction, but plays essentially a passive role. Economic quantities expressed in terms of money do not actuate choice, but serve merely for recording costs and results according to the set goals and modes of production. (Of course, exceptions are the consumer market and choice of employment.)

The centralized directive management system originated in an unfavourable historical context, in circumstances of enemy encirclement and economic backwardness, which posed rapid industrialization as a life and

---

[6] *Planovoye Khozyaystvo*, no. 3/1926, p. 51.

death issue for the first socialist country; the course of strict centralization in planning and management of the Soviet economy was, therefore, unavoidable. But this centralization severely limited the scope for initiative by the enterprises in choosing their means and alternatives, and *khozraschot* was converted by degrees into an instrument of recording and controlling how an enterprise fulfilled the decisions of the authority assigning plan indicators. Consequently, the idea of *khozraschot* as a principle of rational operation within enterprises and throughout the economy was lost to view. It was debased into a mere instrument for signalizing the economic situation of an enterprise. Moreover, its application was reduced to the sphere of industrial enterprises. Application of *khozraschot* in commercial enterprises, where the principle of economic calculation had originated in the past, was regarded as an exception. So on all sides *khozraschot* was debased and restricted.[7] Preliminary calculation likewise assumed a minor role, and any such calculations by enterprises had a negligible effect on decisions at the centre.

Demands on central planning grew enormously. Alongside its chief objective — to indicate the scientifically based course of economic advance, to open up new resources for this advance and coordinate all sectors for the purpose of satisfying society's needs to the maximum with minimum expenditure of social labour — the state plan gradually assumed a new role of applying administrative pressure on enterprises to operate economically, and the means employed were more detailed indicators dictating all aspects of operations. Central and sectoral planning authorities found themselves increasingly obliged to impose "hard targets" and "mobilizing figures" on enterprises, they had more and more often to argue that the plan was feasible, while they themselves were under considerable pressure in the way of

[7] The results of the Soviet discussions in the twenties should be measured against the actual historical situation to which they referred. There was no alternative to centralized decision-making and planning as a means to achieve rapid industrialization under the first Five-Year Plans. But this is far from implying that the economists who take what amounts to the same position of the one-time opponents of the market mechanism are right today. With the present level of the productive forces and the changed international situation, the views quoted acquire full justification and an unadulterated *khozrashchot* becomes fully applicable.

124

demands for allocation of investment resources, materials and manpower. There was a proliferation of autonomous agencies for allocating materials, especially those in short supply, and such methods often took over the role of the universal equivalent – money.

No reorganization, nor extension of records, analyses and check-ups was capable of bridging the widening gap between the interests of the centre and the enterprises. There was no cure, because unity of interests between enterprises and the organs of planned management had been seriously disrupted. And the only source of such unity lies in harnessing commodity and money relations.[8]

This is also one of the leading ideas in the economic reforms being undertaken by one socialist country after another. The point at issue is to

---

[8] "Socialism continually develops, changes and adapts to new conditions, like a living organism. It adapts the organization of socialist production relations, and still more the organization and forms of management, to the development of the productive forces.

These changes bear witness to the crystallization and maturing of socialism as a social order. Forms of highly centralized management and planning belonged to a past phase. They grew out of the possibilities of the past stage, which was typified more by the use of non-economic stimuli, political persuasion and propaganda than by the normal use of economic laws. This is typical for a stage when the new socialist economy does not develop spontaneously from capitalism, but is a conscious and planned goal of the socialist state.

Political revolution changes the social and economic system in the socialist state, the dictatorship of the proletariat is the driving force that remoulds socio-economic relations. This means that the transformation takes place primarily by means of non-economic instruments of coercion, especially by expropriating the capitalists, agricultural reform etc. But simultaneously the socialist state organizes, regulates, appeals to the conscience of the working class and employs a whole range of non-economic, administrative, legal and propagandistic means which have dominated and had to dominate in the transition period. To the extent that socialist society matures, the role of these means declines. They may, indeed, become an obstacle to rational economic operation. The employment of new "models" is founded on forces within the socialist economy and not on a basis of non-economic stimuli. The process assumes different aspects in different countries, but at bottom the trend is the same. The more the new, socialist order matures, the less it needs the help of non-economic stimuli from the state, the more it can stand on its own feet and rely on the working of economic laws." (O. LANGE, *Pisma ekonomiczne i spoleczne 1930–1960*, pp. 58–59.)

lay the basis for thorough-going implementation of the principle of rational operation. *Khozraschot*, which not long ago was still a formal affair, is returning to its original concept. That is to say, economic calculation is being resurrected.

## c) Compromises concerning the model of operation, monopoly structure of the market

To carry out economic reforms is a complicated undertaking which may be threatened by ill-advised compromises. Where a compromise solution is applied, it is usually a matter of simply reforming indicators with the idea of curing the contradictions of the centralized model by various improvements. They do not go beyond the framework of the model. The endeavour to reform indicators in this way has been manifested in two directions. Firstly, in the attempt to find a new basic volume indicator to which material incentives would again be tied and which would simply replace the gross output indicator. Secondly, in the endeavour to tie the incentives of groups (supply personnel, development staff etc.) to performance according to detailed indicators (supplies, technological development etc.)

Today this compromise is quite obviously untenable; essential changes in the management model cannot be exchanged for a mere reform in the basic volume incentive, or a break-down of the entire indicator system to the smallest details.

True, in operating directive management the process of reproduction is recorded in various detailed indicators. But reproduction is such a complicated process that it is impossible to record it effectively from the top and guide it in all its details. In the upshot the detail indicators usually come into conflict. This is all the more true when we realize that the system is not static, but dynamic. The intricate changes in an economy cannot be projected into all the corresponding plan indicators. The result is an aggravation of the contradictions among the detailed indicators of the plan.

The saying goes that "a good planner can put a lot right". But to try and patch up the differences among directive indicators is to skate on thin ice. In fact, much more than adjusting the plan indicators is involved. As we know, the centralized directive model contains built-in contradictions not only between enterprise interests and the directive plan indicators, but also within the system of indicators operative in each enterprise. In this case, if group incentives were to be more firmly tied to individual plan indicators, the more difficult it would be to achieve an "informal", but fairly effective reconciliation of cotradictions in the plan. The employees in each group would concentrate on "their" indicator, which might in the short run yield some results in individual sectors, but in the long term could only aggravate the conflicts.

Following the discussions among Marxist economists in the twenties, whatever the subject, we can distinguish a common concern — from different angles, to resolve the problem of making a socialist economy work in such a way that the principle of rational operation would be realized. Today, the very same problem confronts us — to admit no compromise in applying the principle of rational operation, fully and practically, so that hitherto untapped sources of growth shall be set in motion.

A grave obstacle to attaining economic rationality by bringing enterprise and community interests into better accord is presented by the monopoly structure of the socialist market. This factor could strangle the economic model at birth, to the detriment of growth.

If the new model is to be a leading factor in future development, it is essential that the optimal scope be provided for socialist competitiveness among enterprises of a given branch. But on this point the old attitudes are still widespread, with strong support from executives for whom monopoly is easier than competition. Lenin's maxim that monopoly leads to stagnation cannot, however, be reserved for imperialism alone.

Supposing that a survey were to be made to discover the technological level and quality of commodities and services selected at random from those produced (provided) under conditions of complete monopoly, competition among monopolies or fairly free competition, the result would probably leave little room for doubt. A few contrasts will illustrate the point. As to services, it is interesting to note the standards of hotels, and especially restaurants, for foreign tourists in Czechoslovakia, which have to compete for custom and compare well with those in other countries. Compare, on the other hand, the quality of plumbing services, where the customer is at the mercy of a single concern. The position with consumer goods is obvious enough from the fact that products originally destined for export to competitive markets that have been rejected as defective by the exporters often provide a source of "quality" goods for the home market.

Regarding the scope for competition, a distinction should, however, be made in general between production of capital and consumer goods in respect of the optimal size of enterprises. Obviously, in the first case the degree of association, the present level of concentration, specialization and combination of production severely limit the opportunities for competition and the scope for the market mechanism, and therefore for commodity-money relations. For an enterprise drawing most of its material from a single producer and delivering almost all its products to a single customer, it makes very little difference if inter-enterprise relationships are dubbed socialist commodity relations instead of supplier-buyer relations. In dealings among monopolies conditions are lacking here for effective working of the market mechanism. The economic contacts among monopolies are governed by the relation of forces among them and by government measures. As an object of study they belong more to the sphere of theory of strategic games than of market equilibrium.[9]

In the sphere that can be roughly defined as covering production of consumer goods, commerce and many service branches, the situation is entirely different. The optimal size of enterprises in these sectors gives no cause, either economic or technological, for monopoly formation. Monopolies here are constructed artificially, sometimes by the pressure of group interests, despite that fact that the negative aspects outweigh any considerations of extending the social character of the productive forces.[10]

With the limited effectiveness of administrative price control, specialization, cooperation and production combination taken beyond the degree required by economic and technological considerations are, in reality, expressions of a propensity on the part of pseudo-socialist quasi-cartels to accumulate comfortable monopoly profits and to get rid of undesirable outsiders. Experiences from the early days of the planned economy are relevant

[9]  The limited prospects for using the market mechanism in some heavy industry sectors should not, however, lead to rejecting economic calculation as an instrument of rational operation in all industrial fields. From this angle, economic reform has to take in the entire area of production.

[10]  E. VOPIČKA, *Politická ekonomie*, no. 7/1964, p. 676.

128

here. In many cases, the general directorates of those days inherited along with the headquarters of former cartels the monopoly spirit of their predecessors. The political qualities of the new executives were not at fault, but they were motivated by the economic environment that actually had to be created for them. For the above reasons, it is important, indeed essential, for the success of the new management model, to give the consumer industries, commerce and many services wide opportunities to choose alternative suppliers.

The question of the actual forms in which democratic centralism should be implemented in the planned management of a socialist economy has been posed in various ways. Quite often it is formulated as a matter of direct versus indirect management methods and their linkages, or of administrative versus economic management, or of centralization and decentcentralization. But none of these bracketings is exact. Essentially it is a matter of the plan and the market. When the activities of production units are laid down to the smallest detail, no scope is left for independent decision-making. But if the range of enterprise decision is to be extended, the role of the market has to be increased. The market mechanism is the essential feature of a model capable of replacing the centralized directive model.

However, to increase the role of the market implies giving the consumer the greatest possible opportunity for choice and guaranteeing his sovereignty. In the sphere of consumer goods there are big possibilities waiting to be tapped. As for producer goods, where economically justified monopoly organization is dominant, the only prospect − necessarily a long-term one − is to open up frontiers, primarily within the socialist world.

Seeking the causes of the technological upswing in capitalist monopolies, especially in heavy industry, we find that it was accompanied by a policy of open frontiers, with fierce competition among concerns on foreign and home markets.

The centralized, directive management model encouraged the advance of monopolistic features in the economy, indeed, from the standpoint of allocating production targets and materials, manpower etc., it enforced them. The opposite is true for economic management relying on wide use of the market mechanism. To work effectively, it requires that the broadest possible scope be provided for competition among enterprises.

Moreover, both the given model of planning and management and — primarily — the degree to which the economy is monopolized, directly affect the elasticity of the system, i.e. the speed with which it is capable of adjusting to changing conditions. One of the best analyses of industrial structure has reached an interesting conclusion in this connection from the standpoint of long-term development. The adaptability of the structure is found to carry perhaps as much weight as the actual choice of the structure itself. The centralized, directive model with a high degree of monopoly is capable of bringing about rapid structural changes at the level of sectors, i.e. priority growth of some sectors at the expense of others. But intrasectoral changes, which will be increasingly typical for Czechoslovakia's future industrial development, can be accomplished more easily by a different management system. They can be accomplished within a model that contains no tendencies to the rigidity inherent in directive management, but which will operate under conditions where competition exerts a strong economic pressure on enterprises to adapt promptly to changing conditions on the market.

### d) Effectiveness and so-called structural reform of Czechoslovak industry

From about the beginning of the sixties the attention of some economists has been attracted to the structural problems of Czechoslovak industry. This is on the whole quite natural. Grave signs of disturbance in the economic organism and the impracticability of the structure demanded by the third five-year plan aroused doubts about the suitability of the industrial structure shaped by formerly unquestioned ideas as to "classical" socialist industrialization. Changes in the social background in the latter half of the fifties made it possible — and our difficulties encouraged such enquiry — to take a closer look at the structural trends in western countries. The first comparative studies increased the doubts as to whether the former approaches to setting the structure of industrial production and investments could be maintained.

As the revolutions in science and technology advance they impinge on all elements of production and are manifested in structural changes involving sources of primary energy, construction materials and all types of production materials sectors and branches of production and the entire national economy.

Examination of the industrial structure in economically advanced countries shows that progress is proceeding in roughly the following directions:

— in the sphere of primary resources, the change-over from solid fuels to oil and natural gas is speeding up;
— in the sphere of materials, big savings in the relative consumption of construction materials stem from changes in composition and quality (in metallurgy in favour of sheet metal, formed materials, high-durability steels, metals resistant to high pressures and temperatures), materials substitution (e.g. aluminium and plastics) and progressive technologies (moulding, precision casting, chemical processes);
— man-made fibres and plastics are spreading in the consumer industries:
— industrial structure shows a tendency for production of electric power, engineering and primarily chemicals to outpace the overall growth of industry; extraction of solid fuels records decelerating growth, while the shares of textiles, leather-working and footwear in total industrial production are falling steeply;
— branch structure exhibits a relative advance of the progressive branches (power equipment, electronic and automation parts, transport equipment, shaping machines, measuring instruments, manufacture of fertilizers, man-made materials, medical supplies etc.):
— in the structure of the national economy the movement is towards a relative fall off in the proportion of labour in the primary sector (primary production), stagnation and prospective decline in the secondary (manufacturing) and an upswing in the tertiary sector (expanse of trade and some service branches);
— in the majority of countries rapid growth of the infrastructure is taking place — facilities and institutions required for the effective operation of the productive sectors (transport, communications, health services, education etc.).

A study of the advanced countries where the revolution in science and technology is starting to make itself felt indicates that radical changes in work and the economy of social labour are on the way, with a transformation of living conditions to be expected in the future.

Progressive trends in production and the national economy differ in degree according to the economic maturity of the country concerned, the strength and nature of its ties with the world economy, the traditions, and skill pattern of its labour force and its economically applicable natural resources.

In 1961−2, economic research reached the conclusion that the structure of Czechoslovak industry called for excessively high inputs of investment, materials and labour and that this could not be maintained. This was a valuable contribution to an understanding of the causes underlying the country's economic difficulties.[11]

Structural analyses have indicated that deeper investigation of economic processes is needed. The findings have also underlined the fact that genuine analysis cannot be replaced by a mere confrontation of the plan targets with the degree to which they are met. Such "analyses" have served to detract attention from scientific diagnosis and have sought the causes of our difficulties in the sphere of inadequate fulfilment of planned targets.

However, the fate that has befallen the results of structural analyses is instructive and serves as a warning for scientific undertakings and for practical activity. Some economists have ascribed an absolute value to findings on the production structure and failed to grasp them as a step on the road to deeper understanding of the causes underlying disturbances in the reproduction process. And so we have met in the recent past, and occasionally still meet today, with attempts to explain defects in the structure of production in isolation from overall effectiveness and the management model. The pressure of growing difficulties and the propensity of the man on the job to draw immediate conclusions for practice from every isolated scientific finding − which is both a relic of earlier methods of work and to some extent an attitude inherent in any practical activity − have resulted in findings about the defects in the Czechoslovak industrial structure being the subject of ill-considered slogans, propagating the idea that planning and

[11] Among the most valuable pieces of work of this kind was an "Analysis of the Development of the Czechoslovak Economy" made by a group on the staff of the Research Institute of Economic Planning.

economic practice in general should be directed to a grand new structural reform. There is even talk of a kind of third structural reform comparable in extent and costs to the changes of the early fifties. The very fact that over the years these wishes have led to nothing, either in practice or in long-term plans, intimates that a finding that is not incorporated in an integrated concept of economic correlations may for a time serve as a slogan promising a final solution, but ultimately leads to disorientation both in research and in practical measures.

How then should we view the structural problems of the Czechoslovak economy, especially in the field of industry? The general significance of structural factors in analysing economic development seem liable to overestimation. After all, structural shifts such as were made in Czechoslovakia after 1945 have taken place in the pre- and post-war periods in a strikingly similar way in nearly all advanced capitalist countries without any negative effects on their economic growth (See Table 11).

Table 11. *Comparison of the trend of industrial structure in Czechoslovakia (1948—1957) and in industrially advanced capitalist countries (1921—1956)*

|  | 1948 | 1953 | 1957 | Average annual increment or decrease | Col. 4 in % col. 2 | Corresponding data for capitalist countries |
|---|---|---|---|---|---|---|
| Industry total | 100 | 100 | 100 | . | . | . |
| Mines | 6·2 | 4·2 | 4·1 | −0·23 | −0·50 | −1·30 |
| Power | 2·8 | 2·3 | 2·6 | −0·02 | −0·90 | −0·30 |
| Metallurgy | 9·1 | 9·5 | 9·1 | 0·00 | 0·00 | +0·20 |
| Chemicals | 7·7 | 7·8 | 8·0 | +0·03 | +0·40 | +0·60 |
| Engineerings | 15·5 | 25·9 | 26·6 | +1·23 | +4·70 | +1·80 |
| Textiles | 10·8 | 7·7 | 7·8 | −0·22 | −2·90 | −0·90 |
| Foodstuffs | 22·5 | 21·2 | 19·1 | −0·38 | −1·80 | −1·00 |
| Other | 25·4 | 21·4 | 22·7 | . | . | .00 |

Source: J. FANTL, *Dlouhodobý vývoj struktury průmyslu v hlavních kapitalistických zemích* (Long-term Development of Industrial Structure in the Main Capitalist Countries), UTEIN 1959, pp. 17, 18 (data for power in column 6 added from the authors' figures).

True, there are some differences. However, they do not concern the nature of the structural changes, but the speed with which they were carried out. In the industrial sectors recording a rise (or fall) of their share in the overall industrial production of Czechoslovakia, there was also a rise (fall) in the capitalist countries referred to. The only difference is that the average annual increases (decreases) in the shares of sectors were substantially higher in Czechoslovakia — with the exception of chemicals — than in the other countries.

In this connection it may be noted that the analogy in the trend of the industrial structure holds in part for the capitalist countries poor in raw materials that have experienced "economic miracles". Both in Italy and Japan there has been a remarkable leap forward in such sectors as metallurgy (Table 12). And neither country has experienced any chronic trouble in transforming its surpluses of manufactured goods (and foodstuffs) into raw materials through foreign trade. This would suggest that the root cause of Czechoslovakia's notorious foreign trade barrier does not lie in her industrial structure, but in the inadequacy of her labour productivity. For a country lacking an all-round raw-material base and forced to rely in the main on imports, shortage of raw materials is simply a result of difficulties in selling its manufactures on world markets; where top-quality goods are offered, the necessary raw materials can always be found. The reputed divorce of the Czechoslovak economy from the development of her raw-material base is, in fact, merely a reflection of shortcomings in productivity, in other words, ineffectiveness stemming primarily from the operation of model factors.

Table 12. *Steel production in Italy, Japan and Czechoslovakia 1937 and 1962 (mil. tons)*

|  | 1937 | 1962 | 1962 (1937 = 100) |
|---|---|---|---|
| Italy | 2·1 | 9·5 | 455 |
| Japan | 5·8 | 27·5 | 475 |
| Czechoslovakia | 2·3 | 7·6 | 330 |

**Source:** Statistical yearbooks.

134

The above international comparison (and others) indicate that the problem of proportionality and structural changes is more complicated and needs to be examined in finer categories than those of all-sector indicators. Such an approach would place the structural question in the Czechoslovak economy in a proper light, showing up more clearly the negative consequences flowing from the traditional management model, now operating under conditions so divergent from those obtained at the time it was instituted.

The analysis shows that changes of a branch rather than a sectoral nature are involved. And since products of a given branch can often be processed by the same machines and by people with the same skills, changes of branch structure are less dependent on investment construction than in the case of sectoral shifts. In the former case, flexibility is more important than structural changes requiring extensive investment outlays. The centralized directive system, however, contained strong built-in counter-incentives to changes in production programmes. Consequently, the primary means for accomplishing structural changes at the present stage is offered by the economic system of planning and management, with an appropriate socialist market.

In the light of our analyses we have come to the conclusion that the structure itself is governed by the management model, of which it is in a certain sense a function. Structural troubles are far more strongly connected with the management system than is generally believed. The deleterious effect of the administrative directive system on the structure trend can be seen in three respects. Firstly, inadequate impulses, and not uncommonly counter-incentives, make for high inputs of materials, labour and investment resources. In planning the distribution of investment and manpower resources this appears in the form of exaggerated priorities for some extractive and materials branches, with cuts in investments and labour for other branches. Secondly, the atmosphere created by the system disencourages alertness in applying scientific and technological know-how and promoting innovations in general. Thirdly, the directive plan determines branch and sectoral structures mainly from the standpoint of material balances, and in allocating investment it fails to take proper notice of long-term market trends.

In Chapters IV and V we have dealt in greater detail with the bad effects of the traditional management model on the trend of production costs. Here again a thorough and prompt change in the mechanism of operation is seen as the prime need. Mere structural reforms designed to eliminate the distortions engendered by the old system are not enough. Should the system be allowed to remain, it would again breed structural disproportions.

No one denies the importance of structural changes in the Czechoslovak economy. But in what order of urgency should the problems be taken? Effectiveness takes top place. But effectiveness will not be renewed by a "grand" structural reform. What is needed is a change-over to an economic system of planning and management, revival of economic calculation as an instrument of rational operation. On this basis it will then be possible to resolve the problems properly, without the danger of their emerging later in more serious forms. Investment funds and raw materials, power and labour can all be wasted, both with the present or any other, even the most perfect, structure. It all depends on people and their interests, and on the rules of the game set by the management model adopted.

The idea of a "grand" structural reform derives in part from the habitual outlook of administrative directive management, whereby disproportions are handled by a new manoeuvre and a new campaign. The harm done in economic life by various campaigns has been amply proved on more than one occasion. It has rightly been pointed out that "great leaps" belong to the gymnasium and not to the economy. So hard-won experience warns us against resorting to "great" structural reform and launching a new investment cycle, the consequences of which would put the events of 1953 – 4 and 1961 – 3 completely in the shade.

In the field of technological development, too, the ill effects of the administrative directive system have been felt. The capacity of production to adapt flexibly to new discoveries in science and technology has been weakened. Such discoveries provide a strong stimulus to change in the structure of production, but they can be put into operation as elements of production only through the medium of a given system of economic management. The system creates a more or less favourable atmosphere for the genesis and adoption of scientific findings, and especially for the capacity of production to keep adjusting to the contribution of science.

136

The prime concern of an enterprise under the administrative system is to fulfil the planned volume of output. Enterprises that show initiative and alertness in making use of the latest know-how and in keeping their assortments up to date not only reap no advantages, but quite often are even at a disadvantage compared with those that meet plan targets using existing techniques and accepted technologies. The down-the-line assignment of planned output targets and the incentive system subordinated to it push into the background the leading yardstick of enterprise performance — maximum earnings obtained by satisfying customers' needs to the utmost while minimizing production costs. Only too often the system sets a gulf between scientific discoveries and their practical application, whether it be introduction of new products, improving their qualities, changing over to new production processes, using new tools and materials or reorganizing production. Thanks to the counter incentives to technological advance, progressive innovations even fail to find the place in production foreseen by the central plan and realizable out of means allotted. The principle of rational operation in the long view usually gives way to short-term concern with meeting volume targets.

Furthermore, the administrative system fails to give an adequate impulse to technological advance in modernizing assortments and improving product quality. The rate at which production programmes are changed is low. While on a world scale a single decade (roughly the sixties) saw a hundred-per-cent change in engineering programmes, in Czechoslovakia the figure was only ten per cent (excluding newly-installed programmes). (Data by the State Commission for Science and Technology). The lag in technological development is to be seen in quality falling short of world standards. A check-up in 50 production branches showed that in 1964 about 36 per cent of products were up to or above the world average, some 27 per cent were technologically and otherwise out of date and were due for dropping from production and fully 37 per cent of all products checked were below world standards and in need of progressive substitution or modernization.

Some of the defects in the structure of Czechoslovak production have to do with the method by which the directive plan lays down sectoral and branch structures in advance. A national plan can, in certain circumstances, accomplish structural shifts more rapidly and economically than the price mechanism alone. But the plan in the administrative directive system sets the sectoral and branch structures primarily with a view to material balances and fails to pay adequate attention to the natural, long-term trends of the market. The outcome is an imbalance between the structure of production, preordained by previous investment allocation, and the structure of final needs, which when commodity-money relations are operating is shaped by market forces.

If economic growth is to be balanced, allocation of investments to sectors and branches needs to be economically grounded in such a way that price relations will tend towards the value, or costs relations. A national plan can ensure balanced growth if it respects the allocation function performed by the law of value. This implies a distribution of social labour whereby the rate of profit compared with socially necessary costs is more or less uniform among the branches of production.

Taking the law of value and the price mechanism into account does not signify that the market mechanism should dictate the distribution of investments. It is generally known that the market cannot give a reliable picture of investment effectiveness. Market signals in the guise of fairly long-term fluctuations from price and costs relations — insofar as non-economic considerations have not led to public control — indicate defects in the reproduction process. But disparities in relations between costs and the equilibrium price of the base period are not in themselves decisive for determining the degree of effectiveness of investment in one branch or another. The anticipated price movement has to be taken into account, and this will depend on the trend of supply and demand. Rational investment allocation can be accomplished on the basis of a plan that is a model of the future market and takes into account both equilibrium prices of the base period and the future price dynamics by examining the elasticity of supply and demand.

In the traditional management system, the plan often preordains a production structure conflicting with the future market development and it lacks instruments capable of making a lasting adjustment of investment and production structure to long-term trends in demand. In real life, progressive branches cannot be promoted and structural changes accomplished overnight. There has to be a steady process of adjusting production to economically serviceable advances in science; the structure of investment and production has to be capable of reacting to changing needs. And this takes us from the subject of the current economic structure to its long-term aspects.

"In this respect, the former management system was static, because it lacked an economic feed-back. Every new trend or proportion was given absolute significance and turning points could never meet with a prompt response. With industrialization, the changes occurring from time to time — confined on the whole to the instruments of labour, i.e. tools, machinery and the like — could be carried through by a simple directive transfer of resources to new types of production and by stabilizing some newly-acquired proportions. A hang-over from these days is the conviction that the scientific and technological revolution can be called into being by the selfsame directive methods — by something in the nature of a technocratic procedure. But this stems from a misconception about the substance of the revolution, which is not just a structural shift that can be carried out by one simple operation, but involves a continuous, universal stream of structural changes, with a multidimensional dynamic as the very essence of its progress. Consequently, only a flexible, steadily developing and improving system of planned management, commanding a fully elaborated economic feed-back, can clear the forward road. In order to accomplish 'the full development of the productive forces', — as Marx pointed out — it is not enough for 'certain conditions of production ... to be established'; it is necessary that the dynamics of the productive forces be built in to the social conditions of production, to the structure of interests in human life. Such mobile, regenerating production relations alone allow for a proper appreciation of science and technology, enabling them to be used in a planned way as social productive forces."[12]

Although in the search for the road to Czechoslovakia's economic advance there is apt to be much talk about structural changes, salvation cannot be found either in a steel concept, an upsurge in chemical or in any other great structural reform. Nor does the answer lie in copying the structure of the US or some smaller country, such as Switzerland. In constructing long-range perspectives one cannot start from *a priori* assumptions, thereby exchanging the end for the means. To declare with certainty before the event

---

[12] R. RICHTA, "Dynamika doby a naše revoluce" (Dynamics of the Day and Our Revolution), *Rudé právo*, May 27, 1966.

139

that the long-term plan should speed up the development of one or another sector appears to be a relic of the old exhortatory, campaigning mode of economic management; it harbours the danger of a voluntaristic approach to structural matters.

We may conclude from these considerations that the true guarantee of effective economic development is to be found in replacing the administrative, directive management model by a more suitable model.

Compared with the administrative distribution of production factors, the system of planned management using the law of value and the market mechanism represents a higher type of planning; it affords better opportunities for ensuring stable, balanced economic growth and for shaping the structure on national lines.

# Conclusion

This book has been written at a time when in Czechoslovakia and other socialist countries questions of economic growth at the present stage, and of socialist economic models, have been under discussion. The relevance of the leading ideas in our analysis to these discussions may be stated briefly as follows:

Economic growth is a process involving not only relationships among the different growth parameters, but also correlation of the growth parameters with the model of socialist economic operation. Our work has drawn both on previous research on growth theory and on analyses concerned with models of socialist economic operation. As distinct from research conducted mainly along one line or the other, we have tried to detect the interrelationships in the overall process of economic growth that stem from the influence of the given management system on growth factors and production structure.

The centralized directive system led to degeneration of economic calculation as an instrument of rational operation and its merely formal application. The outcome was deceleration of growth, which is especially evident at a time when the Czechoslovak economy is no longer drawing on accumulation alone. In line with world trends, the role of non-investment growth factors is growing, and the socialist economy offers good conditions for harnessing them. The renaissance of economic calculation in the socialist economy opens the door − given an effective management system − to full application of the principle of rational operation at enterprise level and throughout the national economy.

In the course of debates on the administrative directive system, some stimulating theoretical works have appeared in various socialist countries. What is lacking is quantification of the effectiveness shown by the traditional management system. The present book − following up previous research − represents an attempt to quantify the acceleratory or deceleratory effects of the administrative directive system in the Czechoslovak economy. At the start of the fifties, acceleration effects resulting from overall changes in production relations can be noted. In the early years, investment sources played a smaller part compared with non-investment growth factors; by the latter half of the fifties, they predominated. But in the sixties their effect was offset by deceleration factors, because the administrative directive system retards non-investment growth factors, thereby blocking a quite extensive potential of the Czechoslovak economy.

Both the origin and the widening of the gap between the internal and world price levels were long ignored by economic theory. We have tried here to employ analysis of the disparity as a further instrument in quantifying the influence of the management system of growth processes.

Czechoslovakia's economic growth — as that of some other socialist countries — has shown fluctuations in the growth rates of the national income, industrial production and investment activity. These fluctuations have so far received little attention. Economists have offered various explanations; some have examined the connection between fluctuation and sporadic technological development, and have concluded that wave movement is a normal and permanent feature of economic growth; others link cycles with errors in planning. The analysis presented in this book underlines the relevance of wave movement to the working of the administrative directive management system under conditions given by the concept of economic development adopted.

Some difficulties have accompanied Czechoslovakia's economic course in the sixties. Following fairly high growth rates, a temporary slow-down was evident in 1962—4, and the revival of industrial production and the national income in 1965 and 1966 was not accompanied by adequate advance in labour productivity and overall effectiveness. More detailed enquiries have revealed that the chief obstacle to further progressive advance and a strengthening of socialist production relations is set by a conflict between the present need for economic growth and the out-dated system of management. In recent years, therefore, economic reform, in its theoretical and practical aspects, has engaged the attention of specialists and the general public.

In changing over from the administrative directive system to central planning based on a controlled market mechanism, the socialist countries are breaking new ground. Theoretically and practically, the project has been insufficiently explored. Moreover, Czechoslovakia's move to a higher type of socialist planned management is not being made under the most auspicious circumstances. Harnessing the controlled market mechanism, which is the vital nerve of the economic management model, is severely hampered by the monopoly market structure and the legacy of inflationary pressures that are inherent in the type of economic growth shaped by the traditional system of management. Moreover, there are still some theoretically and practically unresolved questions of price regulation, rational arrangement of socialist economic organizations and, last but not least, knotty problems of foreign trade and external economic relations both with the socialist and capitalist countries. All these circumstances suggest that the first steps now being taken along the path to an economic system will encounter many obstacles and points of conflict; the only chance of success lies in an imaginative development of the economic management system. One cannot exclude prompt remedial measures at points where policies undertaken have not yielded the expected results.

The leading ideas underlying Czechoslovakia's new system of planned management have much in common with the reforms in preparation or under way in most European socialist countries with a view to raising economic efficiency. At the present stage in Czechoslovakia, however, there are circumstances making radical reform and a rapid switch to a more effective system of managing the socialist economy doubly urgent. The country's comparatively high degree of economic advance and satisfaction of needs calls for management capable of readily adapting production structure to changing needs. With sources of new manpower exhausted, growth can be promoted only by methods providing all-round encouragement to technological development. The relatively high degree to which the Czechoslovak economy is geared to world division of labour demands a management system that can raise the effectiveness of foreign trade exchanges.

From this standpoint there is good reason to ask ourselves whether some of the problems of growth and the operative model of the Czechoslovak economy are not pointers to the problems awaiting those socialist countries that in view of their distinct historical backgrounds are still on a rather different economic level.

The Czechoslovak reform of planned management may be regarded as a contribution to the world-wide discussion on how to arrive at an organic linking of the plan with a controlled market mechanism in the context of socialist economic relations. The Czechoslovak road is one of the possible ways of tackling this current problem.

This book will have fulfilled its purpose if it helps to underline the necessity of taking such a road and to point out the snags involved in the complicated process of social-economic change. In recent years economic theory has yielded some valuable results, thanks especially to the spread of fruitful discussion. The work herewith offered to our readers is intended as a contribution to further exchanges of opinion.

# List of Diagrams

# Literature

BOMBACH G.: "Wirtschaftswachstum", *Handwörterbuch der Sozialwissenschaften,* vol. XII.

BRUS W.: *Ogólne problemy funkcjonowania gospodarki socjalistycznej,* Warsaw 1961.

DOMAR E. D.: *Essays in the Theory of Economic Growth,* New York 1957.

*Ekonomia polityczna socjalizmu,* Warsaw 1964, edited by W. Brus.

FELDMAN G. A.: "K teorii temp narodnogo dokhoda", *Planovoye Khozjaystvo,* nos. 11 and 12, 1928.

HARROD R. E.: *Towards a Dynamic Economics,* London 1956.

HORVAT B.: *Towards a Theory of Economic Planning,* Belgrade 1964.

KALECKI G.: *Zarys teorii wzrostu gospodarki socjalistycznej,* Warsaw 1963.

KLEIN L. R.: *Role of Econometrics in Socialist Economics, Problem of Economic Dynamics and Planning,* Warsaw 1964.

KOŽUŠNÍK Č.: *Problémy teorie hodnoty a ceny za socialismu* (Theory of Value and Prices under Socialism), NČSAV, Prague 1964.

KUZNETS S.: *Capital in the American Economy. Its Formation and Financing,* New York 1962.

KUZNETS S.: *Six Lectures on Economic Growth,* New York 1961.

LANGE O.: *Ekonomia polityczna,* Warsaw 1959.

LANGE O.: *Pisma ekonomiczne i społeczne 1930—1960,* Warsaw 1961.

LASKI K.: *Zarys teorii reprodukcji socjalistycznej,* Warsaw 1965.

LUKASIEWICZ A.: *Przyspieszony wzrost gospodarki socjalistycznej w związku z teorię G. Feldmana,* Warsaw 1965.

SAMUELSON P. A.: *Economics,* New York 1964.

SCHUMPETER J. A.: *History of Economic Analysis,* London 1955.

STOJANOVIĆ R.: *Teoria wzrostu gospodarczego w socjalizmie,* Warsaw 1965.

ŠIK O.: *Příspěvek k analýze našeho hospodářského rozvoje* (Contribution to Analysis of Our Economic Development), Research publication, Institute of Economics CAS, No 5, 1965.

# Index

148

149

www.ingramcontent.com/pod-product-compliance
Ingram Content Group UK Ltd.
Pitfield, Milton Keynes, MK11 3LW, UK
UKHW020348010325
455677UK00021B/352